MORALITY

AND THE

LAW

Contemporary Issues

Series Editors: Robert M. Baird
Stuart E. Rosenbaum

MORALITY

AND THE

LAW

edited by: *ROBERT M. BAIRD*
and *STUART E. ROSENBAUM*

PROMETHEUS BOOKS
Buffalo, New York

Published 1988 by Prometheus Books
700 East Amherst Street, Buffalo, New York 14215

2nd Printing 1993

Library of Congress Cataloging-in-Publication Data

Morality and the law / edited by Robert M. Baird and Stuart E. Rosenbaum.
        p. 148   cm.—(Contemporary issues in philosophy)
    Bibliography: p.
    ISBN 0-87975-474-5
    1. Law and ethics. I. Baird, Robert M., 1937-
II. Rosenbaum, Stuart E. III. Series.
BJ55.M594 1988
340'.112—dc19   88-18650
CIP

Printed in the United States of America

Contents

5

6   Contents

Introduction

When Glenda wants to smoke marijuana but society disapproves, what should be done? When the government conscripts John to fight in a war that he judges immoral, what is to be done? These questions confront head-on the oldest and most basic issue in social philosophy: What are the rights of the individual in relationship to society? Conversely, what rights may the collective social body claim in relationship to the individual? When people get together to form a society, how are the respective rights of individuals and the society at large to be structured? It is generally acknowledged that both individuals and the group have legitimate rights that each must recognize, but precisely what those rights are and the limits that restrict their invocation is a matter of continual discussion and debate.

This debate expresses itself in a variety of ways, the most dramatic of which is in the conflict between individual conscience and law. The many questions such conflicts generate include the following: Should morality be legislated (given the force of law)? When conscience and law conflict, which should be obeyed?

The essays in the first part of this volume address the question of whether morality should be legally enforced. The controversial nature of this question is rooted in a simple observation: laws seem to originate in moral convictions. Thus, since it is morally wrong to take someone's life without justification, murder is illegal. But it is by no means clear that all moral convictions of a given society (even those of the majority in a democracy) should be enforced by legal sanctions. Should moral opposition to prostitution, for example, result in laws prohibiting such activity? Which moral convictions should be incorporated into the legal code? Ultimately, one is faced with the need to delineate the proper relationship between morality and law.

The first three selections in Part One involve the widely publicized exchange between Sir Patrick Devlin and H. L. A. Hart. In his Maccabaean Lecture in Jurisprudence, delivered to the British Academy, Devlin responded to the 1957 Report of the Wolfenden Committee, which recommended that the British government liberalize laws concerning homosexuality and prostitution. He took issue with the committee's judgment that the law should not concern itself with private immorality unless the behavior in question "offended against public order and decency or exposed the ordinary citizen to what is offensive or injurious." Arguing that an established morality is essential to social order, Devlin defended the use of law to enforce morality. The suppression of immoral activity, he argued, is as justified as the suppression of political subversion, and for the same reason—the preservation of the community.

Hart, like Devlin, focuses attention on the key question: "Is the fact that certain conduct is by common standards immoral sufficient to justify making that conduct punishable by law?" Objecting to what he calls "legal moralism," Hart defends the Wolfenden Report's claim that "There must remain a realm of private morality and immorality which is, in brief and crude terms, not the law's business." Included here are two essays by Hart that subject Devlin's views to detailed critical analysis. In objecting to Devlin's desire to turn popular morality into criminal law, Hart challenges the claim that individual liberty and personal choice should be limited simply by the moral feelings of others.

In the concluding essay of Part One, Joel Feinberg notes that the legal enforcement of morality is problematic precisely because some immoral conduct may not be socially harmful—certain forms of sexual activity between consenting adults, for example. He discusses several principles often used as justification for limiting the freedom of individuals. These include the *harm principle* (behavior should be prohibited by coercion only if that behavior harms someone else), the *offense principle* (behavior should be coercively prohibited if it is publicly offensive to the moral feelings of others), and the *principle of legal moralism* (immoral behavior should be punished simply because it is immoral). Feinberg believes that in order to characterize the kind of behavior society is justified in controlling, the harm principle must be supplemented by a carefully formulated version of the offense principle.

Part Two focuses on the conflict between individual conscience and the law. Suppose John is convinced that abortions are always morally wrong, but the law permits abortions under any circumstances. If he is to obey his conscience, should John attempt to prohibit women from getting legally permissible abortions? When conscience and law conflict, which is to take precedence?

In this context, consider conscience as simply an individual's convictions about which actions are morally right or wrong, morally good or bad. Thus, to say that a person's conscience is leading him to object to abortion, or that it is telling him that a particular military action is morally wrong, would simply be a figurative way of asserting the person's moral conviction that he ought to oppose abortion or military action. Law in this context is a rule of conduct prescribed by a properly constituted governing authority, enforced by sanctions, and justified by a mandate to legislate for the public good. As some would express it, a law is a rule of conduct that is "on the books."

Given these accounts of conscience and law, a fundamental question arises: When a person is morally convinced that he ought to do one thing, but the legally constituted authority directs otherwise (where the two courses of action are incompatible), what is the individual to do?

Logically it appears that persons who are confronted with this moral dilemma find themselves presented with at least three alternatives: (1) obey the law, even though it conflicts with conscience; (2) follow conscience, even though it conflicts with law; or (3) follow neither of the previous courses, thus choosing to obey the law or follow personal conscience as the particular circumstances require. The third alternative seems to require specifying principles in terms of which the decision is made in any given instance to obey the law or to follow one's conscience.

Before briefly exploring these alternatives, a word about the nature of civil disobedience is appropriate. Most philosophical discussions of civil disobedience characterize it as: (1) a public protest against a governmental law, measure, or policy, or against the acts or policies of some private organization; (2) involving an illegal act, although the specific law or policy violated may not be the one held to be objectionable; (3) nonviolent; (4) motivated by the conviction that the law in question is immoral; and (5) involving an agent who is willing to accept the legal consequences of his action. The widespread acceptance of this understanding of civil disobedience is testimony to the influence of Hugo Bedau, whose well-known discussion of it is included here.

Let us return to the three logical possibilities mentioned above. According to the first, one ought always to obey the law whenever it conflicts with dictates of conscience. This position is defended by Leon Jaworski who argues that to engage in civil disobedience is tantamount to a complete rejection of the rule of law. He holds that judging it acceptable in any situation to violate the law in obedience to conscience makes it impossible ever to justify obeying the law when someone's conscience speaks to the contrary. If obedience to conscience is to take precedence over the rule of law in virtually any situation, then the law serves no real purpose at all. The basic choice, according to Jaworski, is between a society regulated by law and a "new order" that espouses civil disobedience and disrespect for law. The latter choice would result in anarchy.

The extreme position that conflicts between conscience and the law ought always to be settled in favor of the former is not represented in this volume. But the essay by Erich Fromm strongly defends the value of disobedience. Distinguishing between authoritarian and humanistic conscience, he defends obedience to the latter as essential to civilization. Obedience to humanistic conscience may, of course, involve breaking the law, but, Fromm would argue, that is precisely the course of action that, for example, an Adolf Eichmann should have taken.

The third alternative is that of sometimes obeying law and sometimes obeying conscience. The key challenge for this position is to establish guidelines for deciding when to obey one's conscience and when to obey the law. The first two alternatives may be attempts to escape the complexity of this task, and intellectual responsibility may require facing the difficult question: When ought one to obey the law and when ought one to obey conscience? The remaining essays in Part Two grapple with this issue.

Rudolph H. Weingartner denies that there can be any general principle that enables one readily to decide when civil disobedience is justified and when it is not. Each instance of civil disobedience, whether actual or proposed, must be examined separately. Weingartner does argue, however, that there are considerations that should be taken into account when trying to decide whether the disobedience in question is in fact justified.

Charles L. Black, Jr. indicates that his own attitude toward civil disobedience has shifted over the years. Early on he considered it incompatible with the American conception of government under law, but later he modified his view to one that recognized civil disobedience as justified in exceptional circumstances. However, Black does not consider this concession to be incompatible with a commitment to the rule of law. His essay concludes by arguing that much of what has passed as civil disobedience in the United States has not been disobedience at all. Instead, there have occasionally been strong assertions of the priority of national law over state law. Such assertions of priority have actually been means of defending and implementing law.

John Rawls has won wide acclaim and respect for his theory of justice. The principles of justice, he argues, are the principles that would be agreed upon by individuals who had gathered under certain conditions to create a social structure. The following are included among the conditions: (1) all participants would need to be free and rational, (2) they would all have equal powers and rights, and (3) none of them would know the situation or position that would be his or hers in the social order to be created by their choice. Rawls specifies the two crucial principles of justice that he thinks would emerge from what he calls "an original position." The purpose of Rawls's essay is to discuss civil disobedience within the broader context of a just society. A problem arises, he argues, because even a just constitution does not guarantee that the laws generated under it will be just. Moreover, an obligation exists to obey even unjust laws as long as they do not exceed certain limits. But when those limits are exceeded, civil disobedience is justified, and the major thrust of Rawls's essay is to discuss just such an eventuality. He interprets civil disobedience as an address to the community in which it is declared that "in the sincere opinion of the dissenters, the conditions of social cooperation are not being honored."

In the concluding essay, Peter Singer offers a critique of Rawls's position. Singer actually agrees with Rawls's basic claim that civil disobedience is justified under certain circumstances and that such disobedience is compatible with a democratic form of government. Nevertheless, Singer disagrees with certain features of the stance Rawls takes. His essay is therefore a good example of one professional philosopher subjecting another's work to critical analysis.

Having completed the essays in this volume, the reader may well feel that many matters are left open and unresolved. Indeed, they are. But, generally speaking, that is the way of most philosophical discussion. The issues are complex, and relevant facts are often hard to come by. The problems cannot be resolved in any facile way or with the certainty of a simple mathematical equation. The essays presented here do testify, however, to the fact that considerable progress can be made by careful philosophical analysis.

Part One

The Enforcement of Morality

The Enforcement of Morals*

Patrick Devlin

The Report of the Committee on Homosexual Offenses and Prostitution, generally known as the Wolfenden Report, is recognized to be an excellent study of two very difficult legal and social problems. But it has also a particular claim to the respect of those interested in jurisprudence; it does what law reformers so rarely do; it sets out clearly and carefully what in relation to its subjects it considers the function of the law to be.[1] Statutory additions to the criminal law are too often made on the simple principle that "there ought to be a law against it." The greater part of the law relating to sexual offenses is the creation of statute and it is difficult to ascertain any logical relationship between it and the moral ideas which most of us uphold. Adultery, fornication, and prostitution are not, as the Report[2] points out, criminal offenses: homosexuality between males is a criminal offense, but between females it is not. Incest was not an offense until it was declared so by statute only fifty years ago. Does the legislature select these offenses haphazardly or are there some principles which can be used to determine what part of the moral law should be embodied in the criminal? There is, for example, being now considered a proposal to make A.I.D., that is, the practice of artificial insemination of a woman with the seed of a man

From *The Enforcement of Morals* by Patrick Devlin (1965). Copyright 1965 by Oxford University Press. Reprinted in edited form by permission of Oxford University Press.

*Maccabaean Lecture in Jurisprudence read at the British Academy on 18 March 1959 and printed in the *Proceedings of the British Academy,* vol. xiv, under the title "The Enforcement of Morals."

who is not her husband, a criminal offense; if, as is usually the case, the woman is married, this is in substance, if not in form, adultery. Ought it to be made punishable when adultery is not? This sort of question is of practical importance, for a law that appears to be arbitrary and illogical, in the end and after the wave of moral indignation that has put it on the statute book subsides, forfeits respect. As a practical question it arises more frequently in the field of sexual morals than in any other, but there is no special answer to be found in that field. The inquiry must be general and fundamental. What is the connection between crime and sin and to what extent, if at all, should the criminal law of England concern itself with the enforcement of morals and punish sin or immorality as such?

The statements of principle in the Wolfenden Report provide an admirable and modern starting-point for such an inquiry. . . .

Early in the Report[3] the Committee put forward:

Our own formulation of the function of the criminal law so far as it concerns the subjects of this inquiry. In this field, its function, as we see it, is to preserve public order and decency, to protect the citizen from what is offensive or injurious, and to provide sufficient safeguards against exploitation and corruption of others, particularly those who are specially vulnerable because they are young, weak in body or mind, inexperienced, or in a state of special physical, official, or economic dependence.

It is not, in our view, the function of the law to intervene in the private lives of citizens, or to seek to enforce any particular pattern of behavior, further than is necessary to carry out the purposes we have outlined.

The Committee preface their most important recommendation[4]

that homosexual behavior between consenting adults in private should no longer be a criminal offense, [by stating the argument[5]] which we believe to be decisive, namely, the importance which society and the law ought to give to individual freedom of choice and action in matters of private morality. Unless a deliberate attempt is to be made by society, acting through the agency of the law, to equate the sphere of crime with that of sin, there must remain a realm of private morality and immorality which is, in brief and crude terms, not the law's business. To say this is not to condone or encourage private immorality.

Similar statements of principle are set out in the chapters of the Report which deal with prostitution. No case can be sustained, the Report says, for attempting to make prostitution itself illegal.[6] The Committee refer to the general reasons already given and add: "We are agreed that private immorality should not be the concern of the criminal law except in the special circumstances therein mentioned." They quote[7] with approval the report of the Street Offenses Committee,[8] which says: "As a general proposition it will be universally accepted that the law is not concerned with private morals or with ethical sanctions." It will be observed that the emphasis is on *private* immorality. By this is meant immorality which is not offensive or injurious to the public in the ways defined or described in the first passage which I quoted. In other words, no act of immorality should be made a criminal offense unless it is accompanied by some other feature such as indecency, corruption, or exploitation. This is clearly brought in relation to prostitution: "It is not the duty of the law to concern itself with immorality as such . . . it should confine itself to those activities which offend against public order and decency or expose the ordinary citizen to what is offensive or injurious.[9]" . . .

If this view is sound, it means that the criminal law cannot justify any of its provisions by reference to the moral law. It cannot say, for example, that murder and theft are prohibited because they are immoral or sinful. The State must justify in some other way the punishments which it imposes on wrongdoers and a function for the criminal law independent of morals must be found. This is not difficult to do. The smooth functioning of society and the preservation of order require that a number of activities should be regulated. The rules that are made for that purpose and are enforced by the criminal law are often designed simply to achieve uniformity and convenience and rarely involve any choice between good and evil. Rules that impose a speed limit or prevent obstruction on the highway have nothing to do with morals. Since so much of the criminal law is composed of rules of this sort, why bring morals into it at all? Why not define the function of the criminal law in simple terms as the preservation of order and decency and the protection of the lives and property of citizens, and elaborate those terms in relation to any particular subject in the way in which it is done in the Wolfenden Report? The criminal law in carrying out these objects will undoubtedly overlap the moral law. Crimes of violence are morally wrong and they are also offenses against good order; therefore they offend against both laws. But this is simply because the two laws in pursuit of different objectives happen to cover the same area. Such is the argument. . . .

Thus, if the criminal law were to be reformed so as to eliminate from it everything that was not designed to preserve order and decency or to protect citizens (including the protection of youth from corruption), it would overturn a fundamental principle. It would also end a number of specific crimes. Euthanasia or the killing of another at his own request, suicide, attempted suicide and suicide pacts, duelling, abortion, incest between brother and sister, are all acts which can be done in private and without offense to others and need not involve the corruption or exploitation of others. Many people think that the law on some of these subjects is in need of reform, but no one hitherto has gone so far as to suggest that they should all be left outside the criminal law as matters of private morality. They can be brought within it only as a matter of moral principle. It must be remembered also that although there is much immorality that is not punished by the law, there is none that is condoned by the law. The law will not allow its processes to be used by those engaged in immorality of any sort. For example, a house may not be let for immoral purposes; the lease is invalid and would not be enforced. But if what goes on inside there is a matter of private morality and not the law's business, why does the law inquire into it at all?

I think it is clear that the criminal law as we know it is based upon moral principle. In a number of crimes its function is simply to enforce a moral principle and nothing else. The law, both criminal and civil, claims to be able to speak about morality and immorality generally. Where does it get its authority to do this and how does it settle the moral principles which it enforces? Undoubtedly, as a matter of history, it derived both from Christian teaching. But I think that the strict logician is right when he says that the law can no longer rely on doctrines in which citizens are entitled to disbelieve. It is necessary therefore to look for some other source.

In jurisprudence, as I have said, everything is thrown open to discussion and, in the belief that they cover the whole field, I have framed three interrogatories addressed to myself to answer:

1. Has society the right to pass judgement at all on matters of morals? Ought there, in other words, to be a public morality, or are morals always a matter for private judgement?

2. If society has the right to pass judgement, has it also the right to use the weapon of the law to enforce it?

3. If so, ought it to use that weapon in all cases or only in some; and if only in some, on what principles should it distinguish?

I shall begin with the first interrogatory and consider what is meant by the right of society to pass a moral judgement, that is, a judgement about what is good and what is evil. The fact that a majority of people may disapprove of a practice does not of itself make it a matter for society as a whole. Nine men out of ten may disapprove of what the tenth man is doing and still say that it is not their business. There is a case for a collective judgement (as distinct from a large number of individual opinions which sensible people may even refrain from pronouncing at all if it is upon somebody else's private affairs) only if society is affected. Without a collective judgement there can be no case at all for intervention. Let me take as an illustration the Englishman's attitude to religion as it is now and as it has been in the past. His attitude now is that a man's religion is his private affair; he may think of another man's religion that it is right or wrong, true or untrue, but not that it is good or bad. In earlier times that was not so; a man was denied the right to practice what was thought of as heresy, and heresy was thought of as destructive of society.

The language used in the passages I have quoted from the Wolfenden Report suggests the view that there ought not to be a collective judgement about immorality *per se*. Is this what is meant by "private morality" and "individual freedom of choice and action"? Some people sincerely believe that homosexuality is neither immoral nor unnatural. Is the "freedom of choice and action" that is offered to the individual, freedom to decide for himself what is moral or immoral, society remaining neutral; or is it freedom to be immoral if he wants to be? The language of the Report may be open to question, but the conclusions at which the Committee arrive answer this question unambiguously. If society is not prepared to say that homosexuality is morally wrong, there would be no basis for a law protecting youth from "corruption" or punishing a man for living on the "immoral" earnings of a homosexual prostitute, as the Report recommends.[10] This attitude the Committee make even clearer when they come to deal with prostitution. In truth, the Report takes it for granted that there is in existence a public morality which condemns homosexuality and prostitution. What the Report seems to mean by private morality might perhaps be better described as private behavior in matters of morals.

This view—that there is such a thing as public morality—can also be justified by *a priori* argument. What makes a society of any sort is community of ideas, not only political ideas but also ideas about the way its members should behave and govern their lives; these latter ideas are its morals. Every society has a moral structure as well as a political one: or rather, since that might suggest two independent systems, I should say that the structure of every society is made up both of politics and morals. Take, for example, the institution of marriage. Whether a man should be allowed to take more than one wife is something about which every society has to make up its mind one way or the other. In England we believe in the Christian idea of marriage and therefore adopt monogamy as a moral principle. Consequently, the Christian institution of marriage nas become the basis of family life and so part of the structure of our society. It is there not because it is Christian. It has got there because it is Christian, but it remains there because it is built into the house in which we live and could not be removed without bringing it down. The great majority of those who live in this country accept it because it is the Christian idea of marriage and for them the only true one. But a non-Christian is bound by it, not because it is part of Christianity but because, rightly or wrongly, it has been adopted by the society in which he lives. It would be useless for him to stage a debate designed to prove that polygamy was theologically more correct and socially preferable; if he wants to live in the house, he must accept it as built in the way in which it is.

We see this more clearly if we think of ideas or institutions that are purely political. Society cannot tolerate rebellion; it will not allow argument about the rightness of the cause. Historians a century later may say that the rebels were right and the Government was wrong and a percipient and conscientious subject of the State may think so at the time. But it is not a matter which can be left to individual judgement.

The institution of marriage is a good example for my purpose because it bridges the division, if there is one, between politics and morals. Marriage is part of the structure of our society and it is also the basis of a moral code which condemns fornication and adultery. The institution of marriage would be gravely threatened if individual judgements were permitted about the morality of adultery; on these points there must be a public morality. But public morality is not to be confined to those moral principles which support institutions such as marriage. People do not think of monogamy as something which has to be supported because our society has chosen to organize itself upon it; they think of it as something that is good in itself and offering a good way of life and that it is for that reason that our society has adopted it. I return to the statement that I have already made, that society means a community of ideas; without shared ideas on politics, morals, and ethics no society can exist. Each one of us has ideas about what is good and what is evil; they cannot be kept private from the society in which we live. If men and women try to create a society in which there is no fundamental agreement about good and evil they will fail; if, having based it on common agreement, the agreement goes, the society will disintegrate. For society is not something that is kept together physically; it is held by the invisible bonds of common thought. If the bonds were too far relaxed the members would drift apart. A common morality is part of the bondage. The bondage is part of the price of society; and mankind, which needs society, must pay its price.

Common lawyers used to say that Christianity was part of the law of the land. That was never more than a piece of rhetoric as Lord Sumner said in *Bowman* v. *The Secular Society.*[11] What lay behind it was the notion which I have been seeking to expound, namely that morals— and up till a century or so ago no one thought it worth distinguishing between religion and morals—were necessary to the temporal order. In 1675 Chief Justice Hale said: "To say that religion is a cheat is to dissolve all those obligations whereby civil society is preserved."[12] In 1797 Mr. Justice Ashurst said of blasphemy that it was "not only an offense against God but against all law and government from its tendency to dissolve all the bonds and obligations of civil society."[13] By 1908 Mr. Justice Phillimore was able to say: "A man is free to think, to speak, and to teach what he pleases as to religious matters, but not as to morals."[14]

You may think that I have taken far too long in contending that there is such a thing as public morality, a proposition which most people would readily accept, and may have left myself too little time to discuss the next question which to many minds may cause greater difficulty: To what extent should society use the law to enforce its moral judgements? But I believe that the answer to the first question determines the way in which the second should be approached and may indeed very nearly dictate the answer to the second question. If society has no right to make judgements on morals, the law must find some special justification for entering the field of morality: if homosexuality and prostitution are not in themselves wrong, then the onus is very clearly on the lawgiver who wants to frame a law against certain aspects of them to justify the exceptional treatment. But if society has the right to make a judgement and has it on the basis that a recognized morality is as necessary to society as, say, a recognized government, then society may use the law to preserve morality in the same way as it uses it to safeguard anything else that is essential to its existence. If therefore the first proposition is securely established with all its implications, society has a prima facie right to legislate against immorality as such.

The Wolfenden Report, notwithstanding that it seems to admit the right of society to condemn homosexuality and prostitution as immoral, requires special circumstances to be shown to justify the intervention of the law. I think that this is wrong in principle and that any attempt to approach my second interrogatory on these lines is bound to break down. I think that the attempt by the Committee does break down and that this is shown by the fact that it has to define or describe its special circumstances so widely that they can be supported only if it is accepted that the law *is* concerned with immorality as such.

The widest of the special circumstances are described as the provision of "sufficient safeguards against exploitation and corruption of others, particularly those who are specially vulnerable because they are young, weak in body or mind, inexperienced, or in a state of special physical, official, or economic dependence."[15] The corruption of youth is a well-recognized ground for intervention by the State and for the purpose of any legislation the young can easily be defined. But if similar protection were to be extended to every other citizen, there would be no limit to the reach of the law. The "corruption and exploitation of others" is so wide that it could be used to cover any sort of immorality which involves, as most do, the cooperation of another person. Even if the phrase is taken as limited to the categories that are particularized as "specially vulnerable," it is so elastic as to be practically no restriction. This is not merely a matter of words. For if the words used are stretched almost beyond breaking-point, they still are not wide enough to cover the recommendations which the Committee make about prostitution.

Prostitution is not in itself illegal and the Committee do not think that it ought to be made so.[16] If prostitution is private immorality and not the law's business, what concern has the law with the ponce or the brothel-keeper or the householder who permits habitual prostitution? The Report recommends that the laws which make these activities criminal offenses should be maintained or strengthened and brings them (so far as it goes into principle; with regard to brothels it says simply that the law rightly frowns on them) under the head of exploitation.[17] There may be cases of exploitation in this trade, as there are or used to be in many others, but in general a ponce exploits a prostitute no more than an impresario exploits an actress. The Report finds that "the great majority of prostitutes are women whose psychological makeup is such that they choose this life because they find in it a style of living which is to them easier, freer, and more profitable than would be provided by any other occupation. . . . In the main the association between prostitute and ponce is voluntary and operates to mutual advantage."[18] The Committee would agree that this could not be called exploitation in the ordinary sense. They say: "It is in our view an over-simplification to think that those who live on the earnings of prostitution are exploiting the prostitute as such. What they are really exploiting is the whole complex of the relationship between prostitute and customer; they are, in effect, exploiting the human weaknesses which cause the customer to seek the prostitute and the prostitute to meet the demand."[19]

All sexual immorality involves the exploitation of human weaknesses. The prostitute exploits the lust of her customers and the customer the moral weakness of the prostitute. If the exploitation of human weaknesses is considered to create a special circumstance, there is virtually no field of morality which can be defined in such a way as to exclude the law.

I think, therefore, that it is not possible to set theoretical limits to the power of the State to legislate against immorality. It is not possible to settle in advance exceptions to the general rule or to define inflexibly areas of morality into which the law is in no circumstances to be allowed to enter. Society is entitled by means of its laws to protect itself from dangers, whether from within or without. Here again I think that the political parallel is legitimate. The law of treason is directed against aiding the king's enemies and against sedition from within. The justification for this is that established government is necessary for the existence of society and therefore its safety against violent overthrow must be secured.

But an established morality is as necessary as good government to the welfare of society. Societies disintegrate from within more frequently than they are broken up by external pressures. There is disintegration when no common morality is observed and history shows that the loosening of moral bonds is often the first stage of disintegration, so that society is justified in taking the same steps to preserve its moral code as it does to preserve its government and other essential institutions.[20] The suppression of vice is as much the law's business as the suppression of subversive activities; it is no more possible to define a sphere of private morality than it is to define one of private subversive activity. It is wrong to talk of private morality or of the law not being concerned with immorality as such or to try to set rigid bounds to the part which the law may play in the suppression of vice. There are no theoretical limits to the power of the State to legislate against treason and sedition, and likewise I think there can be no theoretical limits to legislation against immorality. You may argue that if a man's sins affect only himself it cannot be the concern of society. If he chooses to get drunk every night in the privacy of his own home, is anyone except himself the worse for it? But suppose a quarter or a half of the population got drunk every night, what sort of society would it be? You cannot set a theoretical limit to the number of people who can get drunk before society is entitled to legislate against drunkenness. The same may be said of gambling. The Royal Commission on Betting, Lotteries, and Gaming took as their test the character of the citizen as a member of society. They said: "Our concern with the ethical significance of gambling is confined to the effect which it may have on the character of the gambler as a member of society. If we were convinced that whatever the degree of gambling this effect must be harmful we should be inclined to think that it was the duty of the state to restrict gambling to the greatest extent practicable."[21]

In what circumstances the State should exercise its power is the third of the interrogatories I have framed. But before I get to it I must raise a point which might have been brought up in any one of the three. How are the moral judgements of society to be ascertained? By leaving it until now, I can ask it in the more limited form that is now sufficient for my purpose. How is the law-maker to ascertain the moral judgements of society? It is surely not enough that they should be reached by the opinion of the majority; it would be too much to require the individual assent of every citizen. English law has evolved and regularly uses a standard which does not depend on the counting of heads. It is that of the reasonable man. He is not to be confused with the rational man. He is not expected to reason about anything and his judgement may be largely a matter of feeling. It is the viewpoint of the man in the street—or to use an archaism familiar to all lawyers—the man in the Clapham omnibus. He might also be called the right-minded man. For my purpose I should like to call him the man in the jury box, for the moral judgement of society must be something about which any twelve men or women drawn at random might after discussion be expected to be unanimous. This was the standard the judges applied in the days before Parliament was as active as it is now and when they laid down rules of public policy. They did not think of themselves as making law but simply as stating principles which every right-minded person would accept as valid. It is what Pollock called "practical morality," which is based not on theological or philosophical foundations but "in the mass of continuous experience half-consciously or unconsciously accumulated and embodied in the morality of common sense." He called it also "a certain way of thinking on questions of morality which we expect to find in a reasonable civilized man or a reasonable Englishman, taken at random."[22]

Immorality then, for the purpose of the law, is what every right-minded person is presumed to consider to be immoral. Any immorality is capable of affecting society injuriously and in effect to a greater or lesser extent it usually does; this is what gives the law its *locus standi*. It cannot be shut out. But—and this brings me to the third question—the individual has a *locus standi* too; he cannot be expected to surrender to the judgement of society the whole conduct of his life. It is the old and familiar question of striking a balance between the rights and interests of society and those of the individual. This is something which the law is constantly doing in matters large and small. To take a very down-to-earth example, let me consider the right of the individual whose house adjoins the highway to have access to it; that means in these days the right to have vehicles stationary in the highway, sometimes for a considerable time if there is a lot of loading or unloading. There are many cases in which the courts have had to balance the private right of access against the public right to use the highway without obstruction. It cannot be done by carving up the highway into public and private areas. It is done by recognizing that each have rights over the whole; that if each were to exercise their rights to the full, they would come into conflict; and therefore that the rights of each must be curtailed so as to ensure as far as possible that the essential needs of each are safeguarded.

I do not think that one can talk sensibly of a public and private morality any more than one can of a public or private highway. Morality is a sphere in which there is a public interest and a private interest, often in conflict, and the problem is to reconcile the two. This does not mean that it is impossible to put forward any general statements about how in our society the balance ought to be struck. Such statements cannot of their nature be rigid or precise; they would not be designed to circumscribe the operation of the law-making power but to guide those who have to apply it. While every decision which a court of law makes when it balances the public against the private is an *ad hoc* decision, the cases contain statements of principle to which the court should have regard when it reaches its decision. In the same way it is possible to make general statements of principle which it may be thought the legislature should bear in mind when it is considering the enactment of laws enforcing morals.

I believe that most people would agree upon the chief of these elastic principles. There must be toleration of the maximum individual freedom that is consistent with the integrity of society. It cannot be said that this is a principle that runs all through the criminal law. Much of the criminal law that is regulatory in character—the part of it that deals with *malum prohibitum* rather than with *malum in se*—is based upon the opposite principle, that is, that the choice of the individual must give way to the convenience of the many. But in all matters of conscience the principle I have stated is generally held to prevail. It is not confined to thought and speech; it extends to action, as is shown by the recognition of the right to conscientious objection in war-time; this example shows also that conscience will be respected even in times of national danger. The principle appears to me to be peculiarly appropriate to all questions of morals. Nothing should be punished by the law that does not lie beyond the limits of tolerance. It is not nearly enough to say that a majority dislike a practice; there must be a real feeling of reprobation. Those who are dissatisfied with the present law on homosexuality often say that the opponents of reform are swayed simply by disgust. If that were so it would be wrong, but I do not think one can ignore disgust if it is deeply felt and not manufactured. Its presence is a good indication that the bounds of toleration are being reached. Not everything is to be tolerated. No society can do without intolerance, indignation, and disgust;[23] they are the forces behind the moral law, and indeed it can be argued that if they or something like them are not present, the feelings of society cannot be weighty enough to deprive the individual of freedom of choice. I suppose that there is hardly anyone nowadays who would not be disgusted by the thought of deliberate cruelty to animals. No one proposes to relegate that or any other form of sadism to the realm of private morality or to allow it to be practiced in public or in private. It would be possible no doubt to point out that until a comparatively short time ago nobody thought very much of cruelty to animals and also that pity and kindliness and the unwillingness to inflict pain are virtues more generally esteemed now than they have ever been in the past. But matters of this sort are not determined by rational argument. Every moral judgement, unless it claims a divine source, is simply a feeling that no right-minded man could behave in any other way without admitting that he was doing wrong. It is the power of a common sense and not the power of reason that is behind the judgements of society. But before a society can put a practice beyond the limits of tolerance there must be a deliberate judgement that the practice is injurious to society. There is, for example, a general abhorrence of homosexuality. We should ask ourselves in the first instance whether, looking at it calmly and dispassionately, we regard it as a vice so abominable that its mere presence is an offense. If that is the genuine feeling of the society in which we live, I do not see how society can be denied the right to eradicate it. Our feeling may not be so intense as that. We may feel about it that, if confined, it is tolerable, but that if it spread it might be gravely injurious; it is in this way that most societies look upon fornication, seeing it as a natural weakness which must be kept within bounds but which cannot be rooted out. It becomes then a question of balance, the danger to society in one scale and the extent of the restriction in the other. On this sort of point the value of an investigation by such a body as the Wolfenden Committee and of its conclusions is manifest.

The limits of tolerance shift. This is supplementary to what I have been saying but of sufficient importance in itself to deserve statement as a separate principle which law-makers have to bear in mind. I suppose that moral standards do not shift; so far as they come from divine revelation they do not, and I am willing to assume that the moral judgements made by a society always remain good for that society. But the extent to which society will tolerate—I mean tolerate, not approve—departures from moral standards varies from generation to generation. It may be that over-all tolerance is always increasing. The pressure of the human mind, always seeking greater freedom of thought, is outwards against the bonds of society forcing their gradual relaxation. It may be that history is a tale of contraction and expansion and that all developed societies are on their way to dissolution. I must not speak of things I do not know; and anyway as a practical matter no society is willing to make provision for its own decay. I return therefore to the simple and observable fact that in matters of morals the limits of tolerance shift. Laws, especially those which are based on morals, are less easily moved. It follows as another good working principle that in any new matter of morals the law should be slow to act. By the next generation the swell of indignation may have abated and the law be left without the strong backing which it needs. But it is then difficult to alter the law without giving the impression that moral judgement is being weakened. This is now one of the factors that is strongly militating against any alteration to the law on homosexuality.

A third elastic principle must be advanced more tentatively. It is that as far as possible privacy should be respected. This is not an idea that has ever been made explicit in the criminal law. Acts or words done or said in public or in private are all brought within its scope without distinction in principle. But there goes with this a strong reluctance on the part of judges and legislators to sanction invasions of privacy in the detection of crime. The police have no more right to trespass than the ordinary citizen has; there is no general right of search; to this extent an Englishman's home is still his castle. The Government is extremely careful in the exercise even of those powers which it claims to be undisputed. Telephone tapping and interference with the mails afford a good illustration of this. A Committee of three Privy Councillors who recently inquired[24] into these activities found that the Home Secretary and his predecessors had already formulated strict rules governing the exercise of these powers and the Committee were able to recommend that they should be continued to be exercised substantially on the same terms. But they reported that the power was "regarded with general disfavor."

This indicates a general sentiment that the right to privacy is something to be put in the balance against the enforcement of the law. Ought the same sort of consideration to play any part in the formation of the law? Clearly only in a very limited number of cases. When the help of the law is invoked by an injured citizen, privacy must be irrelevant; the individual cannot ask that his right to privacy should be measured against injury criminally done to another. But when all who are involved in the deed are consenting parties and the injury is done to morals, the public interest in the moral order can be balanced against the claims of privacy. The restriction on police powers of investigation goes further than the affording of a parallel; it means that the detection of crime committed in private and when there is no complaint is bound to be rather haphazard and this is an additional reason for moderation. These considerations do not justify the exclusion of all private immorality from the scope of the law. I think that, as I have already suggested, the test of "private behavior" should be substituted for "private morality" and the influence of the factor should be reduced from that of a definite limitation to that of a matter to be taken into account. Since the gravity of the crime is also a proper consideration, a distinction might well be made in the case of homosexuality between the lesser acts of indecency and the full offense, which on the principles of the Wolfenden Report it would be illogical to do.

The last and the biggest thing to be remembered is that the law is concerned with the minimum and not with the maximum; there is much in the Sermon on the Mount that would be out of place in the Ten Commandments. We all recognize the gap between the moral law and the law of the land. No man is worth much who regulates his conduct with the sole object of escaping punishment, and every worthy society sets for its members standards which are above those of the law. We recognize the existence of such higher standards when we use expressions such as "moral obligation" and "morally bound." The distinction was well put in the judgement of African elders in a family dispute: "We have power to make you divide the crops, for this is our law, and we will see this is done. But we have not power to make you behave like an upright man."[25]

It can only be because this point is so obvious that it is so frequently ignored. Discussion among law-makers, both professional and amateur, is too often limited to what is right or wrong and good or bad for society. There is a failure to keep separate the two questions I have earlier posed—the question of society's right to pass a moral judgment and the question of whether the arm of the law should be used to enforce the judgement. The criminal law is not a statement of how people ought to behave; it is a statement of what will happen to them if they do not behave; good citizens are not expected to come within reach of it or to set their sights by it, and every enactment should be framed accordingly.

The arm of the law is an instrument to be used by society, and the decision about what particular cases it should be used in is essentially a practical one. Since it is an instrument, it is wise before deciding to use it to have regard to the tools with which it can be fitted and to the machinery which operates it. Its tools are fines, imprisonment, or lesser forms of supervision (such as Borstal and probation) and—not to be ignored—the degradation that often follows upon the publication of the crime. Are any of these suited to the job of dealing with sexual immorality? The fact that there is so much immorality which has never been brought within the law shows that there can be no general rule. It is a matter for decision in each case; but in the case of homosexuality the Wolfenden Report rightly has regard to the views of those who are experienced in dealing with this sort of crime and to those of the clergy who are the natural guardians of public morals.

The machinery which sets the criminal law in motion ends with the verdict and the sentence; and a verdict is given either by magistrates or by a jury. As a general rule, whenever a crime is sufficiently serious to justify a maximum punishment of more than three months, the accused has the right to the verdict of a jury. The result is that magistrates administer mostly what I have called the regulatory part of the law. They deal extensively with drunkenness, gambling, and prostitution, which are matters of morals or close to them, but not with any of the graver moral offenses. They are more responsive than juries to the ideas of the legislature; it may not be accidental that the Wolfenden Report, in recommending increased penalties for solicitation, did not go above the limit of three months. Juries tend to dilute the decrees of Parliament with their own ideas of what should be punishable. Their province of course is fact and not law, and I do not mean that they often deliberately disregard the law. But if they think it is too stringent, they sometimes take a very merciful view of the facts. Let me take one example out of many that could be given. It is an offense to have carnal knowledge of a girl under the age of sixteen years. Consent on her part is no defense; if she did not consent, it would of course amount to rape. The law makes special provision for the situation when a boy and girl are near in age. If a man under twenty-four can prove that he had reasonable cause to believe that the girl was over the age of sixteen years, he has a good defense. The law regards the offense as sufficiently serious to make it one that is triable only by a judge at assizes. "Reasonable cause" means not merely that the boy honestly believed that the girl was over sixteen but also that he must have had reasonable grounds for his belief. In theory it ought not to be an easy defense to make out but in fact it is extremely rare for anyone who advances it to be convicted. The fact is that the girl is often as much to blame as the boy. The object of the law, as judges repeatedly tell juries, is to protect young girls against themselves; but juries are not impressed.

The part that the jury plays in the enforcement of the criminal law, the fact that no grave offense against morals is punishable without their verdict, these are of great importance in relation to the statements of principle that I have been making. They turn what might otherwise be pure exhortation to the legislature into something like rules that the law-makers cannot safely ignore. The man in the jury box is not just an expression; he is an active reality. It will not in the long run work to make laws about morality that are not acceptable to him.

This then is how I believe my third interrogatory should be answered—not by the formulation of hard and fast rules, but by a judgement in each case taking into account the sort of factors I have been mentioning. The line that divides the criminal law from the moral is not determinable by the application of any clear-cut principle. It is like a line that divides land and sea, a coastline of irregularities and indentations. There are gaps and promontories, such as adultery and fornication, which the law has for centuries left substantially untouched. Adultery of the sort that breaks up marriage seems to me to be just as harmful to the social fabric as homosexuality or bigamy. The only ground for putting it outside the criminal law is that a law which made it a crime would be too difficult to enforce; it is too generally regarded as a human weakness not suitably punished by imprisonment. All that the law can do with fornication is to act against its worst manifestations; there is a general abhorrence of the commercialization of vice, and that sentiment gives strength to the law against brothels and immoral earnings. There is no logic to be found in this. The boundary between the criminal law and the moral law is fixed by balancing in the case of each particular crime the pros and cons of legal enforcement in accordance with the sort of considerations I have been outlining. The fact that adultery, fornication, and lesbianism are untouched by the criminal law does not prove that homosexuality ought not to be touched. The error of jurisprudence in the Wolfenden Report is caused by the search for some single principle to explain the division between crime and sin. The Report finds it in the principle that the criminal law exists for the protection of individuals; on this principle fornication in private between consenting adults is outside the law and thus it becomes logically indefensible to bring homosexuality between consenting adults in private within it. But the true principle is that the law exists for the protection of society. It does not discharge its function by protecting the individual from injury, annoyance, corruption, and exploitation; the law must protect also the institutions and the community of ideas, political and moral, without which people cannot live together. Society cannot ignore the morality of the individual any more than it can his loyalty; it flourishes on both and without either it dies. . . .

Society cannot live without morals. Its morals are those standards of conduct which the reasonable man approves. A rational man, who is also a good man, may have other standards. If he has no standards at all he is not a good man and need not be further considered. If he has standards, they may be very different; he may, for example, not disapprove of homosexuality or abortion. In that case he will not share in the community morality; but that should not make him deny that it is a social necessity. A rebel may be rational in thinking that he is right but he is irrational if he thinks that society can leave him free to rebel.

A man who concedes that morality is necessary to society must support the use of those instruments without which morality cannot be maintained. The two instruments are those of teaching, which is doctrine, and of enforcement, which is the law. . . .

NOTES

1. The Committee's "statement of juristic philosophy" (to quote Lord Pakenham) was considered by him in a debate in the House of Lords on 4 December 1957, reported in *Hansard Lords Debates*, vol. ccvi at 738; and also in the same debate by the Archbishop of Canterbury at 753 and Lord Denning at 806. The subject has also been considered by Mr. J. E. Hall Williams in the *Law Quarterly Review*, January 1958, vol. lxxiv, p. 76.

2. Para. 14.
3. Para. 13.
4. Para. 62.
5. Para. 61.
6. Para. 224.
7. Para. 227.
8. Cmd. 3232 (1928).
9. Para. 257.
10. Para. 76.
11. (1917), A.C. 406, at 457.
12. *Taylor's Case*, I Vent. 293.
13. *R. v. Williams*, 26 St. Tr. 653, at 715.
14. *R. v. Boulter*, 72 J. P. 188.
15. Para. 13.
16. Paras. 224, 285, and 318.
17. Paras. 302 and 320.
18. Para. 223.
19. Para. 306.
20. It is somewhere about this point in the argument that Professor Hart in *Law, Liberty and Morality* discerns a proposition which he describes as central to my thought. He states the proposition and his objection to it as follows (p. 51). "He appears to move from the acceptable proposition that *some* shared morality is essential to the existence of any society [this I take to be the proposition on p. 12] to the unacceptable proposition that a society is identical with its morality as that is at any given moment of its history, so that a change in its morality is tantamount to the destruction of a society. The former proposition might be even accepted as a necessary rather than an empirical truth depending on a quite plausible definition of society as a body of men who hold certain moral views in common. But the latter proposition is absurd. Taken strictly, it would prevent us saying that the morality of a given society had changed, and would compel us instead to say that one society had disappeared and another one taken its place. But it is only on this absurd criterion of what it is for the same society to continue to exist that it could be asserted without evidence that any deviation

from a society's shared morality threatens its existence." In conclusion (p. 82) Professor Hart condemns the whole thesis in the lecture as based on "a confused definition of what a society is."

I do not assert that *any* deviation from a society's shared morality threatens its existence any more than I assert that *any* subversive activity threatens its existence. I assert that they are both activities which are capable in their nature of threatening the existence of society so that neither can be put beyond the law.

For the rest, the objection appears to me to be all a matter of words. I would venture to assert, for example, that you cannot have a game without rules and that if there were no rules there would be no game. If I am asked whether that means that the game is "identical" with the rules, I would be willing for the question to be answered either way in the belief that the answer would lead to nowhere. If I am asked whether a change in the rules means that one game has disappeared and another has taken its place, I would reply probably not, but that it would depend on the extent of the change.

Likewise I should venture to assert that there cannot be a contract without terms. Does this mean that an "amended" contract is a "new" contract in the eyes of the law? I once listened to an argument by an ingenious counsel that a contract, because of the substitution of one clause for another, had "ceased to have effect" within the meaning of a statutory provision. The judge did not accept the argument; but if most of the fundamental terms had been changed, I daresay he would have done.

The proposition that I make in the text is that if (as I understand Professor Hart to agree, at any rate for the purposes of the argument) you cannot have a society without morality, the law can be used to enforce morality as something that is essential to a society. I cannot see why this proposition (whether it is right or wrong) should mean that morality can never be changed without the destruction of society. If morality is changed, the law can be changed. Professor Hart refers (p. 72) to the proposition as "the use of legal punishment to freeze into immobility the morality dominant at a particular time in a society's existence." One might as well say that the inclusion of a penal section into a statute prohibiting certain acts freezes the whole statute into immobility and prevents the prohibitions from ever being modified.

These points are elaborated in the sixth lecture at pp. 115–16.

21. (1951) Cmd. 8190, para. 159.

22. *Essays in Jurisprudence and Ethics* (1881), Macmillan, pp. 278 and 353.

23. These words which have been much criticized, are considered again in the Preface at p. viii.

24. (1957) Cmd. 283.

25. A case in the Saa-Katengo Kuta at Lialiu, August 1942, quoted in *The Judicial Process among the Barotse of Northern Rhodesia* by Max Gluckman, Manchester University Press, 1955, p. 172.

The Legal Enforcement of Morality

H. L. A. Hart

These lectures are concerned with one question about the relations between law and morals. I say, advisedly, "one question," because in the heat of the controversy often generated when law and morals are mentioned in conjunction, it is often overlooked that there is not just one question concerning their relations but many different questions needing quite separate consideration. So I shall start by distinguishing four such questions and identifying the one with which I shall be here concerned.

The first is a historical and a causal question: Has the development of the law been influenced by morals? The answer to this question plainly is "Yes"; though of course this does not mean that an affirmative answer may not also be given to the converse question: Has the development of morality been influenced by law? This latter question has scarcely been adequately investigated yet, but there are now many admirable American and English studies of the former question. These exhibit the manifold ways in which morality has determined the course of the law, sometimes covertly and slowly through the judicial process, sometimes openly and abruptly through legislation. I shall say no more here about this historical causal question, except to utter the warning that the affirmative answer which may be given to it, and to its converse, does not mean that an affirmative answer is to be given to other quite different questions about the relations of law and morals.

Reprinted from *Law, Liberty and Morality* by H. L. A. Hart (1963), with changes, with the permission of the publishers, Stanford University Press. Copyright © 1963 by the Board of trustees of the Leland Stanford Junior University.

The second question may be called an analytical or definitional one. Must some reference to morality enter into an adequate definition of law or legal system? Or is it just a contingent fact that law and morals often overlap (as in their common proscription of certain forms of violence and dishonesty) and that they share a common vocabulary of rights, obligations, and duties? These are famous questions in the long history of the philosophy of law, but perhaps they are not so important as the amount of time and ink expended upon them suggests. Two things have conspired to make discussion of them interminable or seemingly so. The first is that the issue has been clouded by use of grand but vague words like "Positivism" and "Natural Law." Banners have been waved and parties formed in a loud but often confused debate. Secondly, amid the shouting, too little has been said about the criteria for judging the adequacy of a definition of law. Should such a definition state what, if anything, the plain man intends to convey when he uses the expressions "law" or "legal system"? Or should it rather aim to provide, by marking off certain social phenomena from others, a classification useful or illuminating for theoretical purposes?

A third question concerns the possibility and the forms of the moral criticism of law. Is law open to moral criticism? Or does the admission that a rule is a valid legal rule preclude moral criticism or condemnation of it by reference to moral standards or principles? Few perhaps of this audience would find any contradiction or paradox in the assertion that a rule of law was valid and yet conflicted with some binding moral principle requiring behavior contrary to that demanded by the legal rule. Yet in our own day Kelsen[1] has argued that there is a logical contradiction in such an assertion, unless it is interpreted merely as an autobiographical statement or psychological report by the speaker of his divergent inclinations both to obey the law and to disobey it by following the moral principle.

Within this third question there are many subordinate ones. Even if we admit, as most would, the possibility of a moral criticism of law, we may ask whether there are any forms of moral criticism which are uniquely or exclusively relevant to law. Does criticism in terms of Justice exhaust all the relevant forms? Or does "good law" mean something different from and wider than "just law"? Is Justice, as Bentham seems to have thought, merely a name for the efficient distribution of Utility or Welfare, or is it otherwise reducible to them? Plainly the adequacy of Utilitarianism as a moral critique of social institutions is in issue here.

The fourth question is the subject of these lectures. It concerns the legal enforcement of morality and has been formulated in many different ways: Is the fact that certain conduct is by common standards immoral sufficient to justify making that conduct punishable by law? Is it morally permissible to enforce morality as such? Ought immorality as such to be a crime?

To this question John Stuart Mill gave an emphatic negative answer in his essay *On Liberty* one hundred years ago, and the famous sentence in which he frames this answer expresses the central doctrine of his essay. He said, "The only purpose for which power can rightfully be exercised over any member of a civilized community against his will is to prevent harm to others.["]2 And to identify the many different things which he intended to exclude, he added, "His own good either physical or moral is not a sufficient warrant. He cannot rightfully be compelled to do or forbear because it will be better for him to do so, because it will make him happier, because in the opinions of others, to do so would be wise or even right.["]3

This doctrine, Mill tells us, is to apply to human beings only "in the maturity of their faculties": it is not to apply to children or to backward societies. Even so, it has been the object of much academic criticism on two different, and indeed inconsistent, grounds. Some critics have urged that the line which Mill attempts to draw between actions with which the law may interfere and those with which it may not is illusory. "No man is an island"; and in an organized society it is impossible to identify classes of actions which harm no one or no one but the individual who does them. Other critics have admitted that such a division of actions may be made, but insist that it is merely dogmatic on Mill's part to limit legal coercion to the class of actions which harm others. There are good reasons, so these critics claim, for compelling conformity to social morality and for punishing deviations from it even when these do not harm others.

I shall consider this dispute mainly in relation to the special topic of sexual morality where it seems *prima facie* plausible that there are actions immoral by accepted standards and yet not harmful to others. But to prevent misunderstanding I wish to enter a *caveat;* I do not propose to defend all that Mill said; for I myself think there may be grounds justifying the legal coercion of the individual other than the prevention of harm to others. But on the narrower issue relevant to the enforcement of morality Mill seems to me to be right. It is of course possible simply to assert that the legal enforcement by society of its accepted morality needs no argument to justify it, because it is a morality which is enforced. But Mill's critics have not fallen back upon this brute assertion. They have in fact advanced many different arguments to justify the enforcement of morality, but these all, as I shall attempt to show, rest on unwarranted assumptions as to matters of fact, or on certain evaluations whose plausibility, due in large measure to ambiguity or vagueness or inaccuracy of statement, dwindles (even if it does not altogether vanish) when exposed to critical scrutiny.

In England in the last few years the question whether the criminal law should be used to punish immorality "as such" has acquired a new practical importance; for there has, I think, been a revival there of what might be termed *legal moralism*. Judges both in their judicial capacity and in extra-judicial statements have gone out of their way to express the view that the enforcement of sexual morality is a proper part of the law's business—as much its business, so one judge has argued, as the suppression of treason. . . .

PROSTITUTION AND HOMOSEXUALITY

. . . Much dissatisfaction has for long been felt in England with the criminal law relating to both prostitution and homosexuality, and in 1954 the committee well known as the Wolfenden Committee was appointed to consider the state of the law. This Committee reported in September 1957[4] and recommended certain changes in the law on both topics. As to homosexuality they recommended by a majority of 12 to 1 that homosexual practices between consenting adults in private should no longer be a crime; as to prostitution they unanimously recommended that, though it should not itself be made illegal, legislation should be passed "to drive it off the streets" on the ground that public soliciting was an offensive nuisance to ordinary citizens. . . .

What concerns us here is less the fate of the Wolfenden Committee's recommendations than the principles by which these were supported. These are strikingly similar to those expounded by Mill in his essay *On Liberty*. Thus section 13 of the Committee's Report reads:

[The] function [of the criminal law], as we see it, is to preserve public order and decency, to protect the citizen from what is offensive or injurious and to provide sufficient safeguards against exploitation or corruption of others, particularly those who are specially vulnerable because they are young, weak in body or mind or inexperienced. . . .

This conception of the positive functions of the criminal law was the Committee's main ground for its recommendation concerning prostitution that legislation should be passed to suppress the offensive public manifestations of prostitution, but not to make prostitution itself illegal. Its recommendation that the law against homosexual practices between consenting adults in private should be relaxed was based on the principle stated simply in section 61 of the Report as follows: "There must remain a realm of private morality and immorality which is, in brief and crude terms, not the law's business."

It is of some interest that these developments in England have had near counterparts in America. In 1955 the American Law Institute published with its draft Model Penal Code a recommendation that all consensual relations between adults in private should be excluded from the scope of the criminal law. Its grounds were (*inter alia*) that "no harm to the secular interests of the community is involved in atypical sex practice in private between consenting adult partners";[5] and "there is the fundamental question of the protection to which every individual is entitled against state interference in his personal affairs when he is not hurting others."[6] This recommendation had been approved by the Advisory Committee of the Institute but rejected by a majority vote of its Council. The issue was therefore referred to the annual meeting of the Institute at Washington in May 1955, and the recommendation, supported by an eloquent speech of the late Justice Learned Hard, was, after a hot debate, accepted by a majority of 35 to 24.[7]

It is perhaps clear from the foregoing that Mill's principles are still very much alive in the criticism of law, whatever their theoretical deficiencies may be. But twice in one hundred years they have been challenged by two masters of the Common Law. The first of these was the great Victorian judge and historian of the Criminal Law, James Fitzjames Stephen. His criticism of Mill is to be found in the sombre and impressive book *Liberty, Equality, Fraternity*,[8] which he wrote as a direct reply to Mill's essay *On Liberty*. It is evident from the tone of this book that Stephen thought he had found crushing arguments against Mill and had demonstrated that the law might justifiably enforce morality as such or, as he said, that the law should be "a persecution of the grosser forms of vice."[9] Nearly a century later, on the publication of the Wolfenden Committee's report, Lord Devlin, now a member of the House of Lords and a most distinguished writer on the criminal law, in his essay on *The Enforcement of Morals*[10] took as his target the Report's contention "that there must be a realm of morality and immorality which is not the law's business" and argued in opposition to it that "the suppression of vice is as much the law's business as the suppression of subversive activities."

Though a century divides these two legal writers, the similarity in the general tone and sometimes in the detail of their arguments is very great. I shall devote the remainder of these lectures to an examination of them. I do this because, though their arguments are at points confused, they certainly still deserve the compliment of rational opposition. They are not only admirably stocked with concrete examples, but they express the considered views of skilled, sophisticated lawyers experienced in the administration of the criminal law. Views such as theirs are still quite widely held especially by lawyers both in England and in this country; it may indeed be that they are more popular, in both countries, than Mill's doctrine of Liberty.

POSITIVE AND CRITICAL MORALITY

Before we consider the detail of these arguments, it is, I think, necessary to appreciate three different but connected features of the question with which we are concerned.

In all the three formulations given on page 34 [of the present volume] it is plain that the question is one *about* morality, but it is important to observe that it is also itself a question *of* morality. It is the question whether the enforcement of morality is morally justified; so morality enters into the question in two ways. The importance of this feature of the question is that it would plainly be no sufficient answer to show that in fact in some society—our own or others—it was widely regarded as morally quite right and proper to enforce, by legal punishment, compliance with the accepted morality. No one who seriously debates this question would regard Mill as refuted by the simple demonstration that there are some societies in which the generally shared morality endorses its own enforcement by law, and does so even in those cases where the immorality was thought harmless to others. The existence of societies which condemn association between white and colored persons as immoral and punish it by law still leaves our question to be argued. It is true that Mill's critics have often made much of the fact that English law does in several instances, apparently with the support of popular morality, punish immorality as such, especially in sexual matters; but they have usually admitted that this is where the argument begins, not where it ends. I shall indeed later claim that the play made by some legal writers with what they treat as examples of the legal enforcement of morality "as such" is sometimes confused. But they do not, at any rate, put forward their case as simply proved by pointing to these social facts. Instead they attempt to base their own conclusion that it is morally justifiable to use the criminal law in this way on principles which they believe to be universally applicable, and which they think are either quite obviously rational or will be seen to be so after discussion.

Thus Lord Devlin bases his affirmative answer to the question on the quite general principle that it is permissible for any society to take the steps needed to preserve its own existence as an organized society,[11] and he thinks that immorality—even private sexual immorality—may, like treason, be something which jeopardizes a society's existence. Of course many of us may doubt this general principle, and not merely the suggested analogy with treason. We might wish to argue that whether or not a society is justified in taking steps to preserve itself must depend both on what sort of society it is and what the steps to be taken are. If a society were mainly devoted to the cruel persecution of a racial or religious minority, or if the steps to be taken included hideous tortures, it is arguable that what Lord Devlin terms the "disintegration"[12] of such a society would be morally better than its continued existence, and steps ought not to be taken to preserve it. Nonetheless Lord Devlin's principle that a society may take the steps required to preserve its organized existence is not itself tendered as an item of English popular morality, deriving its cogency from its status as part of our institutions. He puts it forward as a principle, rationally acceptable, to be used in the evaluation or criticism of social institutions generally. And it is surely clear that anyone who holds the question whether a society has the "right" to enforce morality, or whether it is morally permissible for any society to enforce its morality by law, to be discussable at all, must be prepared to deploy some such general principles of critical morality.[13] In asking the question, we are assuming the legitimacy of a standpoint which permits criticism of the institutions of any society, in the light of general principles and knowledge of the facts.

To make this point clear, I would revive the terminology much favored by the Utilitarians of the last century, which distinguished "positive morality," the morality actually accepted and shared by a given social group, from the general moral principles used in the criticism of actual social institutions including positive morality. We may call such general principles "critical morality" and say that our question is one of critical morality about the legal enforcement of positive morality.

A second feature of our question worth attention is simply that it is a question of *justification*. In asking it we are committed at least to the general critical principle that the use of legal coercion by any society calls for justification as something *prima facie* objectionable to be tolerated only for the sake of some countervailing good. For where there is no *prima facie* objection, wrong, or evil, men do not ask for or give *justifications* of social practices, though they may ask for and give *explanations* of these practices or may attempt to demonstrate their value.

It is salutary to inquire precisely what it is that is *prima facie* objectionable in the legal enforcement of morality; for the idea of legal enforcement is in fact less simple than is often assumed. It has two different but related aspects. One is the actual punishment of the offender. This characteristically involves depriving him of liberty of movement or of property or of association with family or friends, or the infliction upon him of physical pain or even death. All these are things which are assumed to be wrong to inflict on others without special justification, and in fact they are so regarded by the law and morality of all developed societies. To put it as a lawyer would, these are things which, if they are not justified as sanctions, are delicts or wrongs.

The second aspect of legal enforcement bears on those who may never offend against the law, but are coerced into obedience by the threat of legal punishment. This rather than physical restrictions is what is normally meant in the discussion of political arrangements by restrictions on liberty. Such restrictions, it is to be noted, may be thought of as calling for justification for several quite distinct reasons. The unimpeded exercise by individuals of free choice may be held a value in itself with which it is *prima facie* wrong to interfere; or it may be thought valuable because it enables individuals to experiment—even with living—and to discover things valuable both to themselves and to others. But interference with individual liberty may be thought an evil requiring justification for simpler, utilitarian reasons; for it is itself the infliction of a special form of suffering—often very acute—on those whose desires are frustrated by the fear of punishment. This is of particular importance in the case of laws enforcing a sexual morality. They may create misery of a quite special degree. For both the difficulties involved in the repression of sexual impulses and the consequences of repression are quite different from those involved in the abstention from "ordinary" crime. Unlike sexual impulses, the impulse to steal or to wound or even kill is not, except in a minority of mentally abnormal cases, a recurrent and insistent part of daily life. Resistance to the temptation to commit these crimes is not often, as the suppression of sexual impulses generally is, something which affects the development or balance of the individual's emotional life, happiness, and personality.

Thirdly, the distinction already made, between positive morality and principles of critical morality, may serve to dissipate a certain misunderstanding of the question and to clarify its central point. It is sometimes said that the question is not whether it is morally justifiable to enforce morality as such, but only *which* morality may be enforced. Is it only a utilitarian morality condemning activities which are harmful to others? Or is it a morality which also condemns certain activities whether they are harmful or not? This way of regarding the question misrepresents the character of, at any rate, modern controversy. A utilitarian who insists that the law should only punish activities which are harmful adopts this as a critical principle, and, in so doing, he is quite unconcerned with the question whether a utilitarian morality is or is not already accepted as the positive morality of the society to which he applies his critical principles. If it is so accepted, that is not, in his view, the reason why it should be enforced. It is true that if he is successful in preaching his message to a given society, members of it will then be compelled to behave as utilitarians in certain ways, but these facts do not mean that the vital difference between him and his opponent is only as to the content of the morality to be enforced. For as may be seen from the main criticisms of Mill, the Utilitarian's opponent, who insists that it is morally permissible to enforce morality as such, believes that the mere fact that certain rules or standards of behavior enjoy the status of a society's positive morality is the reason—or at least part of the reason—which justifies their enforcement by law. No doubt in older controversies the opposed positions were different: the question may have been whether the state could punish only activities causing secular harm or also acts of disobedience to what were believed to be divine commands or prescriptions of Natural Law. But what is crucial to the dispute in its modern form is the significance to be attached to the historical fact that certain conduct, no matter what, is prohibited by a positive morality. The utilitarian denies that this has any significance sufficient to justify its enforcement; his opponent asserts that it has. These are divergent critical principles which do not differ merely over the content of the morality to be enforced, but over a more fundamental and, surely, more interesting issue.

NOTES

1. Hans Kelsen, *General Theory of Law and State,* pp. 374-76, 407-10.
2. *On Liberty,* Chapter 1.
3. Ibid.
4. Report of the Committee on Homosexual Offences and Prostitution (CMD 247) 1957.
5. American Law Institute Model Penal Code, Tentative Draft No. 4, p. 277.
6. Ibid., p. 278.
7. An account of the debate is given in *Time,* May 30, 1955, p. 13.
8. 2nd edition, London, 1874.
9. Ibid., p. 162.
10. Oxford University Press, 1959.
11. *The Enforcement of Morals,* pp. 13-14.
12. Ibid., pp. 14-15.
13. Lord Devlin has been criticised for asking the question whether society has a *right* to enforce its judgment in matters of morality on the ground that to talk of "right" in such a context is meaningless. See Graham Hughes, "Morals and the Criminal Law," 71 *Yale L.J.* (1962) at 672. This criticism is mistaken, just because Lord Devlin invokes some general critical principle in support of his affirmative answer to the question.

Immorality and Treason

H. L. A. Hart

The most remarkable feature of Sir Patrick Devlin's lecture is his view of the nature of morality—the morality which the criminal law may enforce. Most previous thinkers who have repudiated the liberal point of view have done so because they thought that morality consisted either of divine commands or of rational principles of human conduct discoverable by human reason. Since morality for them had this elevated divine or rational status as the law of God or reason, it seemed obvious that the state should enforce it, and that the function of human law should not be merely to provide men with the opportunity for leading a good life, but actually to see that they lead it. Sir Patrick does not rest his repudiation of the liberal point of view on these religious or rationalist conceptions. Indeed much that he writes reads like an abjuration of the notion that reasoning or thinking has much to do with morality. English popular morality has no doubt its historical connection with the Christian religion: "That," says Sir Patrick, "is how it got there." But it does not owe its present status or social significance to religion any more than to reason.

What, then, is it? According to Sir Patrick it is primarily a matter of feeling. "Every moral judgment," he says, "is a feeling that no right-minded man could act in any other way without admitting that he was doing wrong." Who then must feel this way if we are to have what

"Immorality and Treason" originally appeared in *The Listener* (July 30, 1959), pp. 162-163, and it is reprinted here by permission of the publisher.

Sir Patrick calls a public morality? He tells us that it is "the man in the street," "the man in the jury box," or (to use the phrase so familiar to English lawyers) "the man on the Clapham omnibus." For the moral judgments of society so far as the law is concerned are to be ascertained by the standards of the reasonable man, and he is not to be confused with the rational man. Indeed, Sir Patrick says "he is not expected to reason about anything and his judgment may be largely a matter of feeling."

INTOLERANCE, INDIGNATION, AND DISGUST

But what precisely are the relevant feelings, the feelings which may justify use of the criminal law? Here the argument becomes a little complex. Widespread dislike of a practice is not enough. There must, says Sir Patrick, be "a real feeling of reprobation." Disgust is not enough either. What is crucial is a combination of intolerance, indignation, and disgust. These three are the forces behind the moral law, without which it is not "weighty enough to deprive the individual of freedom of choice." Hence there is, in Sir Patrick's outlook, a crucial difference between the mere adverse moral judgment of society and one which is inspired by feeling raised to the concert pitch of intolerance, indignation, and disgust.

This distinction is novel and also very important. For on it depends the weight to be given to the fact that when morality is enforced individual liberty is necessarily cut down. Though Sir Patrick's abstract formulation of his views on this point is hard to follow, his examples make his position fairly clear. We can see it best in the contrasting things he says about fornication and homosexuality. In regard to fornication, public feeling in most societies is not now of the concert-pitch intensity. We may feel that it is tolerable if confined: only its spread might be gravely injurious. In such cases the question whether individual liberty should be restricted is for Sir Patrick a question of balance between the danger to society in the one scale, and the restriction of the individual in the other. But if, as may be the case with homosexuality, public feeling is up to concert pitch, if it expresses a "deliberate judgment" that a practice as such is injurious to society, if there is "a genuine feeling that it is a vice so abominable that its mere presence is an offense," then it is beyond the limits of tolerance, and society may eradicate it. In this case, it seems, no further balancing of the claims of individual liberty is to be done, though as a matter of prudence the legislator should remember that the popular limits of tolerance may shift: the concert pitch feeling may subside. This may produce a dilemma for the law; for the law may then be left without the full moral backing that it needs, yet it cannot be altered without giving the impression that the moral judgment is being weakened.

A SHARED MORALITY

If this is what morality is—a compound of indignation, intolerance, and disgust—we may well ask what justification there is for taking it, and turning it as such, into criminal law with all the misery which criminal punishment entails. Here Sir Patrick's answer is very clear and simple. A collection of individuals is not a society; what makes them into a society is among other things a shared or public morality. This is as necessary to its existence as an organized government. So society may use the law to preserve its morality like anything else essential to it. "The suppression of vice is as much the law's business as the suppression of subversive activities." The liberal point of view which denies this is guilty of "an error in jurisprudence": for it is no more possible to define an area of private morality than an area of private subversive activity. There can be no "theoretical limits" to legislation against immorality just as there are no such limits to the power of the state to legislate against treason and sedition.

Surely all this, ingenious as it is, is misleading. Mill's formulation of the liberal point of view may well be too simple. The grounds for interfering with human liberty are more various than the single criterion of "harm to others" suggests: cruelty to animals or organizing prostitution for gain do not, as Mill himself saw, fall easily under the description of harm to others. Conversely, even where there is harm to others in the most literal sense, there may well be other principles limiting the extent to which harmful activities should be repressed by law. So there are multiple criteria, not a single criterion, determining when human liberty may be restricted. Perhaps this is what Sir Patrick means by a curious distinction which he often stresses between theoretical and practical limits. But with all its simplicities the liberal point of view is a better guide than Sir Patrick to clear thought on the proper relation of morality to the criminal law: for it stresses what he obscures—namely, the points at which thought is needed before we turn popular morality into criminal law.

SOCIETY AND MORAL OPINION

No doubt we would all agree that a consensus of moral opinion on certain matters is essential if society is to be worth living in. Laws against murder, theft, and much else would be of little use if they were not supported by a widely diffused conviction that what these laws forbid is also immoral. So much is obvious. But it does not follow that everything to which the moral vetoes of accepted morality attach is of equal importance to society; nor is there the slightest reason for thinking of morality as a seamless web: one which will fall to pieces carrying society with it, unless all its emphatic vetoes are enforced by law. Surely even in the face of the moral feeling that is up to concert pitch—the trio of intolerance, indignation, and disgust—we must pause to think. We must ask a question at two different levels which Sir Patrick never clearly enough identifies or separates. First, we must ask whether a practice which offends moral feeling is harmful, independently of its repercussion on the general moral code. Secondly, what about repercussion on the moral code? Is it really true that failure to translate this item of general morality into criminal law will jeopardize the whole fabric of morality and so of society?

We cannot escape thinking about these two different questions merely by repeating to ourselves the vague nostrum: "This is part of public morality and public morality must be preserved if society is to exist." Sometimes Sir Patrick seems to admit this, for he says in words which both Mill and the Wolfenden Report might have used, that there must be the maximum respect for individual liberty consistent with the integrity of society. Yet this, as his contrasting examples of fornication and homosexuality show, turns out to mean only that the immorality which the law may punish must be generally felt to be intolerable. This plainly is no adequate substitute for a reasoned estimate of the damage to the fabric of society likely to ensue if it is not suppressed.

Nothing perhaps shows more clearly the inadequacy of Sir Patrick's approach to this problem than his comparison between the suppression of sexual immorality and the suppression of treason or subversive activity. Private subversive activity is, of course, a contradiction in terms because "subversion" means overthrowing government, which is a public thing. But it is grotesque, even where moral feeling against homosexuality is up to concert pitch, to think of the homosexual behavior of two adults in private as in any way like treason or sedition either in intention or effect. We can make it *seem* like treason only if we assume that deviation from a general moral code is bound to affect that code, and to lead not merely to its modification but to its destruction. The analogy could begin to be plausible only if it was clear that offending against this item of morality was likely to jeopardize the whole structure. But we have ample evidence for believing that people will not abandon morality, will not think any better of murder, cruelty, and dishonesty, merely because some private sexual practice which they abominate is not punished by the law.

Because this is so the analogy with treason is absurd. Of course "No man is an island": what one man does in private, if it is known, may affect others in many different ways. Indeed it may be that deviation from general sexual morality by those whose lives, like the lives of many homosexuals, are noble ones and in all other ways exemplary will lead to what Sir Patrick calls the shifting of the limits of tolerance. But if this has any analogy in the sphere of government it is not the overthrow of ordered government, but a peaceful change in its form. So we may listen to the promptings of common sense and of logic, and say that though there could not logically be a sphere of private treason there is a sphere of private morality and immorality.

Sir Patrick's doctrine is also open to a wider, perhaps a deeper, criticism. In his reaction against a rationalist morality and his stress on feeling, he has I think thrown out the baby and kept the bath water; and the bath water may turn out to be very dirty indeed. When Sir Patrick's lecture was first delivered *The Times* greeted it with these words: "There is a moving and welcome humility in the conception that society should not be asked to give its reason for refusing to tolerate what in its heart it feels intolerable." This drew from a correspondent in Cambridge the retort: "I am afraid that we are less humble than we used to be. We once burnt old women because, without giving our reasons, we felt in our hearts that witchcraft was intolerable."

This retort is a bitter one, yet its bitterness is salutary. We are not, I suppose, likely, in England, to take again to the burning of old women for witchcraft or to punishing people for associating with those of a different race or color, or to punishing people again for adultery. Yet if these things were viewed with intolerance, indignation, and disgust, as the second of them still is in some countries, it seems that on Sir Patrick's principles no rational criticism could be opposed to the claim that they should be punished by law. We could only pray, in his words, that the limits of tolerance might shift.

CURIOUS LOGIC

It is impossible to see what curious logic has led Sir Patrick to this result. For him a practice is immoral if the thought of it makes the man on the Clapham omnibus sick. So be it. Still, why should we not summon all the resources of our reason, sympathetic understanding, as well as critical intelligence, and insist that before general moral feeling is turned into criminal law it is submitted to scrutiny of a different kind from Sir Patrick's? Surely, the legislator should ask whether the general morality is based on ignorance, superstititon, or misunderstanding; whether there is a false conception that those who practice what it condemns are in other ways dangerous or hostile to society; and whether the misery to many parties, the blackmail and the other evil consequences of criminal punishment, especially for sexual offenses, are well understood. It is surely extraordinary that among the things which Sir Patrick says are to be considered before we legislate against immorality these appear nowhere; not even as "practical considerations," let alone "theoretical limits." To any theory which, like this one, asserts that the criminal law may be used on the vague ground that the preservation of morality is essential to society and yet omits to stress the need for critical scrutiny, our reply should be: "Morality, what crimes may be committed in thy name!"

As Mill saw, and de Tocqueville showed in detail long ago in his critical but sympathetic study of democracy, it is fatally easy to confuse the democratic principle that power should be in the hands of the majority with the utterly different claim that the majority, with power in their hands, need respect no limits. Certainly there is a special risk in a democracy that the majority may dictate how all should live. This is the risk we run, and should gladly run; for it is the price of all that is so good in democratic rule. But loyalty to democratic principles does not require us to maximize this risk: yet this is what we shall do if we mount the man in the street on the top of the Clapham omnibus and tell him that if only he feels sick enough about what other people do in private to demand its suppression by law no theoretical criticism can be made of his demand.

Hard Cases for the Harm Principle

Joel Feinberg

MORAL OFFENSES AND LEGAL MORALISM

Immoral conduct is no trivial thing, and we should hardly expect societies to tolerate it; yet if men are *forced* to refrain from immorality, their own choices will play very little role in what they do, so that they can hardly develop critical judgment and moral traits of a genuinely praiseworthy kind. Thus legal enforcement of morality seems to pose a dilemma. The problem does not arise if we assume that all immoral conduct is socially harmful, for immoral conduct will then be prohibited by law not just to punish sin or to "force men to be moral," but rather to prevent harm to others. If, however, there are forms of immorality that do not necessarily cause harm, "the problem of the enforcement of morality" becomes especially acute.

The central problem cases are those criminal actions generally called "morals offenses."* Offenses against morality and decency have long constituted a category of crimes (as distinct from offenses against the person, offenses against property, and so on). These have included mainly sex offenses, such as adultery, fornication, sodomy, incest, and prostitution, but also a miscellany of nonsexual offenses, including cruelty to animals,

Joel Feinberg, *Social Philosophy,* copyright © 1973, pp. 36-45. Reprinted by permission of Prentice Hall, Inc., Englewood Cliffs, New Jersey.

*Previously Feinberg has introduced the "offense principle," the principle that mere offensiveness to morality and decency (as contrasted with causing harm, in the narrow sense of harm) is a ground for preventive coercion in some circumstances.

desecration of the flag or other venerated symbols, and mistreatment of corpses. In a useful article,[1] Louis B. Schwartz maintains that what sets these crimes off as a class is not their special relation to morality (murder is also an offense against morality, but it is not a "morals offense") but the lack of an essential connection between them and social harm. In particular, their suppression is not required by the public security. Some morals offenses may harm the perpetrators themselves, but the risk of harm of this sort has usually been consented to in advance by the actors. Offense to other parties, when it occurs, is usually a consequence of perpetration of the offenses *in public,* and can be prevented by statutes against "open lewdness," or "solicitation" in public places. That still leaves "morals offenses" committed by consenting adults in private. Should they really be crimes?

In addition to the general presumption against coercion, other arguments against legislation prohibiting private and harmless sexual practices are drawn from the harm principle itself; laws governing private affairs are extremely awkward and expensive to enforce, and have side effects that are invariably harmful. Laws against homosexuality, for example, can only be occasionally and randomly enforced, and this leads to the inequities of selective enforcement and opportunities for blackmail and private vengeance. Moreover, "the pursuit of homosexuals involves policemen in degrading entrapment practices, and diverts attention and effort"[2] from more serious (harmful) crimes of aggression, fraud, and corruption.

These considerations have led some to argue against statutes that prohibit private immorality, but, not surprisingly, it has encouraged others to abandon their exclusive reliance on the harm and/or offense principles, at least in the case of morals offenses. The alternative principle of "legal moralism" has several forms. In its more moderate version it is commonly associated with the views of Patrick Devlin,[3] whose theory, as I understand it, is really an application of the public harm principle. The proper aim of criminal law, he agrees, is the prevention of harm, not merely to individuals, but also (and primarily) to society itself. A shared moral code, Devlin argues, is a necessary condition for the very existence of a community. Shared moral convictions function as "invisible bonds" tying individuals together into a orderly society. Moreover, the fundamental unifying morality (to switch the metaphor) is a kind of "seamless web";[4] to damage it at one point is to weaken it throughout. Hence, society has as much right to protect its moral code by legal coercion as it does to protect its equally indispensable political institutions. The law cannot tolerate politically revolutionary activity, nor can it accept activity that rips assunder its moral fabric. "The suppression of vice is as much the law's business as the suppression of subversive activities; it is no more possible to define a sphere of private morality than it is to define one of private subversive activity."[5]

H. L. A. Hart finds it plausible that some shared morality is necessary to the existence of a community, but criticizes Devlin's further contention "that a society is identical with its morality as that is at any given moment of its history, so that a change in its morality is tantamount to the destruction of a society."[6] Indeed, a moral critic might admit that we can't exist as a society without some morality, while insisting that we can perfectly well exist without *this* morality, (if we put a better one in its place). Devlin seems to reply that the shared morality *can* be changed even though protected by law, and, when it does change, the emergent reformed morality in turn deserves *its* legal protection.[7] The law then functions to make moral reform difficult, but there is no preventing change where reforming zeal is fierce enough. How does one bring about a change in prevailing moral beliefs when they are enshrined in law? Presumably by advocating conduct which is in fact illegal, by putting into public practice what one preaches, and by demonstrating one's sincerity by marching proudly off to jail for one's convictions:

> there is . . . a natural respect for opinions that are sincerely held. When such opinions accumulate enough weight, the law must either yield or it is broken. In a democratic society . . . there will be a strong tendency for it to yield—not to abandon all defenses so as to let in the horde, but to give ground to those who are prepared to fight for something that they prize. To fight may be to suffer. A willingness to suffer is the most convincing proof of sincerity. Without the law there would be no proof. The law is the anvil on which the hammer strikes.[8]

In this remarkable passage, Devlin has discovered another argument for enforcing "morality as such," and incidentally for principled civil disobedience as the main technique for initiating and regulating moral change. A similar argument, deriving from Samuel Johnson and applying mainly to changes in religious doctrine, was well known to Mill. According to this theory, religious innovators deserve to be persecuted, for persecution allows them to prove their mettle and demonstrate their disinterested good faith, while their teachings, insofar as they are true, cannot be hurt, since truth will always triumph in the end. Mill held this method of testing truth, whether in science, religion, or morality, to be both uneconomical and ungenerous.[9] But if self-sacrificing civil disobedience is *not* the most efficient and humane remedy for the moral reformer, what instruments of moral change are available to him? This question is not only difficult to answer in its own right, it is also the rock that sinks Devlin's favorite analogy between "harmless" immorality and political subversion.

Consider the nature of subversion. Most modern law-governed countries have a constitution, a set of duly constituted authorities, and a body of statutes created and enforced by these authorities. The ways of changing these things will be well known, orderly, and permitted by the constitution. For example, constitutions are amended, legislators are elected, and new legislation is introduced. On the other hand, it is easy to conceive of various sorts of unpermitted and disorderly change— through assassination and violent revolution, or bribery and subornation, or the use of legitimately won power to extort and intimidate. Only these illegitimate methods of change can be called "subversion." But here the analogy between positive law and positive morality begins to break down. There is no "moral constitution," no well-known and orderly way of introducing moral legislation to duly constituted moral legislators, no clear convention of majority rule. Moral subversion, if there is such a thing, must consist in the employment of disallowed techniques of change instead of the officially permitted "constitutional" ones. It consists not simply of change as such, but of illegitimate change. Insofar as the notion of legitimately induced moral change remains obscure, illegitimate moral change is no better. Still, there is enough content to both notions to preserve some analogy to the political case. A citizen works *legitimately* to change public moral beliefs when he openly and forthrightly expresses his own dissent, when he attempts to argue, persuade, and offer reasons, and when he lives according to his own convictions with persuasive quiet and dignity, neither harming others nor offering counterpersuasive offense to tender sensibilities. A citizen attempts to change mores by *illegitimate* means when he abandons argument and example for force and fraud. If this is the basis of the distinction between legitimate and illegitimate techniques of moral change, then the use of state power to affect moral belief *one way or the other,* when harmfulness is not involved, is a clear example of illegitimacy. Government enforcement of the conventional code is not to be called "moral subversion," of course, because it is used on behalf of the status quo; but whether conservative or innovative, it is equally in defiance of our "moral constitution" (if anything is).

The second version of legal moralism is the pure version, not some other principle in disguise. Enforcement of morality as such and the attendant punishment of sin are not justified as means to some further social aim (such as preservation of social cohesiveness) but are ends in themselves. Perhaps J. F. Stephen was expressing this pure moralism when he wrote that "There are acts of wickedness so gross and outrageous that . . . [protection of others apart], they must be prevented at any cost to the offender and punished if they occur with exemplary severity."[10] From his examples it is clear that Stephen had in mind the very acts that are called "morals offenses" in the law.

It is sometimes said in support of pure legal moralism that the world as a whole would be a better place without morally ugly, even "harmlessly immoral," conduct, and that our actual universe is intrinsically worse for having such conduct in it. The threat of punishment, the argument continues, deters such conduct. Actual instances of punishment not only back up the threat, and thus help keep future moral weeds out of the universe's garden, they also erase past evils from the universe's temporal record by "nullifying" them, or making it as if they never were. Thus punishment, it is said, contributes to the intrinsic value of the universe in two ways: by canceling out past sins and preventing future ones.[11]

There is some plausibility in this view when it is applied to ordinary harmful crimes, especially those involving duplicity or cruelty, which really do seem to "set the universe out of joint." It is natural enough to think of repentance, apology, or forgiveness as "setting things straight," and of punishment as a kind of "payment" or a wiping clean of the moral slate. But in cases where it is natural to resort to such analogies, there is not only a rule infraction, there is also a *victim*—some person or society of persons who have been harmed. Where there is no victim— and especially where there is no profit at the expense of another—"setting things straight" has no clear intuitive content.

Punishment may yet play its role in the discouraging harmless private immoralities for the sake of "the universe's moral record." But if fear of punishment is to keep people from illicit intercourse (or from desecrating flags, or mistreating corpses) in the privacy of their own rooms, then morality shall have to be enforced with a fearsome efficiency that shows no respect for individual privacy. If private moralities are to be deterred by threat of punishment, the detecting authorities must be able to look into the hidden chambers and locked rooms of anyone's private domicile. When we put this massive forfeiture of privacy into the balance along with the usual costs of coercion—loss of spontaneity, stunting of rational powers, anxiety, hypocrisy, and the rest—the price of securing mere outward conformity to the community's moral standards (for that is all that can be achieved by the penal law) is exorbitant.

Perhaps the most interesting of the nonsexual morals offenses, and the most challenging case for application of liberty-limiting principles, is cruelty to animals. Suppose that John Doe is an intelligent, sensitive person with one very severe neurotic trait—he loves to see living things suffer pain. Fortunately, he never has occasion to torture human beings (he would genuinely regret that), for he can always find an animal for the purpose. For a period he locks himself in his room every night, draws the blind, and then beats and tortures a dog to death. The sounds of shrieks and moans, which are music to his ears, are nuisances to his neighbors, and when his landlady discovers what he has been doing she is so shocked she has to be hospitalized. Distressed that he has caused harm to human beings, Doe leaves the rooming house, buys a five hundred acre ranch, and moves into a house in the remote, unpopulated center of his own property. There, in the perfect privacy of his home, he spends every evening maiming, torturing, and beating to death his own animals.

What are we to say of Doe's bizarre behavior? We have three alternatives. First we can say that it is perfectly permissible since it consists simply in a man's destruction of his own property. How a man disposes in private of his own property is no concern of anyone else providing he causes no nuisance such as loud noises and evil smells. Second, we can say that this behavior is patently immoral even though it causes no harm to the interests of anyone other than the actor; further, since it obviously should *not* be permitted by the law, this is a case where the harm principle is inadequate and must be supplemented by legal moralism. Third, we can extend the harm principle to animals, and argue that the law can interfere with the private enjoyment of property not to enforce "morality as such," but rather to prevent harm to the animals.

The third alternative is the most inviting, but not without its difficulties. We *must* control animal movements, exploit animal labor, and, in many cases, deliberately slaughter animals. All these forms of treatment would be "harm" if inflicted on human beings, but cannot be allowed to count as harm to animals if the harm principle is to be extended to them in a realistic way. The best compromise is to recognize one supreme interest of animals, namely the interest in freedom from cruelty or wantonly inflicted pain, and to count as "harm" all and only invasions of *that* interest.

OBSCENITY AND THE OFFENSE PRINCIPLE

Up to this point we have considered the harm and offense principles together in order to determine whether between them they are sufficient to regulate conventional immoralities, or whether they need help from a further independent principle, legal moralism. Morals offenses were treated as essentially private so that the offense principle could not be stretched to apply to them. Obscene literature and pornographic displays would appear to be quite different in this respect. Both are materials deliberately published for the eyes of others, and their existence can bring partisans to the unsupplemented harm principle into direct conflict with those who endorse *both* the harm and offense principles.

In its untechnical, prelegal sense, the word "obscenity" refers to material dealing with nudity, sex, or excretion in an offensive manner. Such material becomes obscene in the legal sense when, because of its offensiveness or for some other reason [this question had best be left open in the definition], it is or ought to be without legal protection. The legal definition then incorporates the everyday sense, and essential to both is the requirement that the material be *offensive*. An item may offend one person and not another. "Obscenity," if it is to avoid this subjective relativity, must involve an interpersonal objective sense of "offensive." Material must be offensive by prevailing community standards that are public and well known, or be such that it is apt to offend virtually everyone.

Not all material that is generally offensive need also be harmful in any sense recognized by the harm principle. It is partly an empirical question whether reading or witnessing obscene material causes social harm; reliable evidence, even of a statistical kind, of causal connections between obscenity and antisocial behavior is extremely hard to find.[12] In the absence of clear and decisive evidence of harmfulness, the American Civil Liberties Union insists that the offensiveness of obscene material cannot be a sufficient ground for its repression:

> . . . the question in a case involving obscenity, just as in every case involving an attempted restriction upon free speech, is whether the words or pictures are used in such circumstances and are of such a nature as to create a clear and present danger that they will bring about a substantial evil that the state has a right to prevent. . . . We believe that under the current state of knowledge, there is grossly insufficient evidence to show that obscenity brings about *any* substantive evil.[13]

The A.C.L.U. argument employs *only* the harm principle among liberty-limiting principles, and treats literature, drama, and painting as forms of expression subject to the same rules as expressions of opinion. In respect to both types of expression, "every act of deciding what should be barred carries with it a danger to the community."[14] The suppression itself is an evil to the author who is squelched. The power to censor and punish involves risks that socially valuable material will be repressed along with the "filth." The overall effect of suppression, the A.C.L.U. concludes, is almost certain to discourage nonconformist and eccentric expression generally. In order to override these serious risks, there must be in a given case an even more clear and present danger that the obscene material, if not squelched, will cause even greater harm; such counter-vailing evidence is never forthcoming. (If such evidence were to accumulate, the A.C.L.U. would be perfectly willing to change its position on obscenity.)

The A.C.L.U. stand on obscenity seems clearly to be the position dictated by the unsupplemented harm principle and its corollary, the clear and present danger test. Is there any reason at this point to introduce the offense principle into the discussion? Unhappily, we may be forced to if we are to do justice to all of our particular intuitions in the most harmonious way. Consider an example suggested by Professor Schwartz. By the provisions of the new Model Penal Code, he writes, "a rich homosexual may not use a billboard on Times Square to promulgate to the general populace the techniques and pleasures of sodomy."[15] If the notion of "harm" is restricted to its narrow sense, that is, contrasted with "offense," it will be hard to reconstruct a rationale for this prohibition based on the harm principle. There is unlikely to be evidence that a lurid and obscene public poster in Times Square would create a clear and present danger of injury to those who fail to avert their eyes in time as they come blinking out of the subway stations. Yet it will be surpassingly difficult for even the most dedicated liberal to advocate freedom of expression in a case of this kind. Hence, if we are to justify coercion in this case, we will likely be driven, however reluctantly, to the offense principle.

There is good reason to be "reluctant" to embrace the offense principle until driven to it by an example like the above. People take perfectly genuine offense at many socially useful or harmless activities, from commercial advertisements to inane chatter. Moreover, widespread irrational prejudices can lead people to be digusted, shocked, even morally repelled by perfectly innocent activities, and we should be loath to permit their groundless repugnance to override the innocence. The offense principle, therefore, must be formulated very precisely and applied in accordance with carefully formulated standards so as not to open the door to wholesale and intuitively unwarranted repression. At the very least we should require that the prohibited conduct or material be of the sort apt to offend almost everybody and not just some shifting majority or special interest group.

It is instructive to note that a strictly drawn offense principle would not only justify prohibition of conduct and pictured conduct that is in its inherent character repellent, but also conduct and pictured conduct that is inoffensive in itself but offensive in inappropriate circumstances. I have in mind so-called indecencies such as public nudity. One can imagine an advocate of the unsupplemented harm principle arguing against the public nudity prohibition on the grounds that the sight of a naked body does no one any harm, and the state has no right to impose standards of dress or undress on private citizens. How one chooses to dress, after all, is a form of self-expression. If we do not permit the state to bar clashing colors or bizarre hair styles, by what right does it prohibit total undress? Perhaps the sight of naked people could at first lead to riots or other forms of antisocial behavior, but that is precisely the sort of contingency for which we have police. If we don't take away a person's right of free speech for the reason that its exercise may lead others to misbehave, we cannot in consistency deny his right to dress or undress as he chooses for the same reason.

There may be no answering this challenge on its own ground, but the offense principle provides a ready rationale for the nudity prohibition. The sight of nude bodies in public places is for almost everyone acutely *embarrassing*. Part of the explanation no doubt rests on the fact that nudity has an irresistible power to draw the eye and focus the thought on matters that are normally repressed. The conflict between these attracting and repressing forces is exciting, upsetting, and anxiety-producing. In some persons it will create at best a kind of painful turmoil, and at worst that experience of exposure to oneself of "peculiarly sensitive, intimate, vulnerable aspects of the self"[16] which is called *shame*. "One's feeling is involuntarily exposed openly in one's face; one is uncovered . . . taken by surprise . . . made a fool of."[17] The result is not mere "offense," but a kind of psychic jolt that in many normal people can be a painful wound. Even those of us who are better able to control our feelings might well resent the *nuisance* of having to do so.

If we are to accept the offense principle as a supplement to the harm principle, we must accept two corollaries which stand in relation to it similarly to the way in which the clear and present danger test stands to the harm principle. The first, the *standard of universality,* has already been touched upon. For the offensiveness (disgust, embarrassment, outraged sensibilities, or shame) to be sufficient to warrant coercion, it should be the reaction that could be expected from almost any person chosen at random from the nation as a whole, regardless of sect, faction, race, age, or sex. The second is the *standard of reasonable avoidability.* No one has a right to protection from the state against offensive experiences if he can effectively avoid those experiences with no unreasonable effort or inconvenience. If a nude person enters a public bus and takes a seat near the front, there may be no effective way for other patrons to avoid intensely shameful embarrassment (or other insupportable feelings) short of leaving the bus, which would be an unreasonable inconvenience. Similarly, obscene remarks over a loudspeaker, homosexual billboards in Times Square, and pornographic handbills thrust into the hands of passing pedestrians all fail to be reasonably avoidable.

On the other hand, the offense principle, properly qualified, can give no warrant to the suppression of *books* on the grounds of obscenity. When printed words hide decorously behind covers of books sitting passively on bookstore shelves, their offensiveness is easily avoided. The contrary view is no doubt encouraged by the common comparison of obscenity with "smut," "filth," or "dirt." This in turn suggests an analogy to nuisance law, which governs cases where certain activities create loud noises or terrible odors offensive to neighbors, and "the courts must weigh the gravity of the nuisance [substitute "offense"] to the neighbors against the social utility [substitute "redeeming social value"] of the defendant's conduct."[18] There is, however, one vitiating disanalogy in this comparison. In the case of "dirty books" the offense is easily avoidable. There is nothing like the evil smell of rancid garbage oozing right out through the covers of a book. When an "obscene" book sits on a shelf, who is there to be offended? Those who want to read it for the sake of erotic stimulation presumably will not be offended (or else they wouldn't read it), and those who choose not to read it will have no experience by which to be offended. If its covers are too decorous, some innocents may browse through it by mistake and be offended by what they find, but they need only close the book to escape the offense. Even this offense, minimal as it is, could be completely avoided by prior consultation of trusted book reviewers. I conclude that there are no sufficient grounds derived either from the harm or offense principles for suppressing obscene literature, unless that ground be the protection of children; but I can think of no reason why restrictions on sales to children cannot work as well for printed materials as they do for cigarettes and whiskey. . . .

NOTES

1. Louis B. Schwartz, "Morals Offenses and the Model Penal Code," *Columbia Law Review,* LXIII (1963), pp. 669 ff.

2. Schwartz, "Morals Offenses and the Model Penal Code," p. 671.

3. Patrick Devlin, *The Enforcement of Morals* (London: Oxford University Press, 1965).

4. The phrase is not Devlin's but that of his critic, H. L. A. Hart, in *Law, Liberty, and Morality* (Stanford: Stanford University Press, 1963), p. 51. In his rejoinder to Hart, Devlin writes: "Seamlessness presses the simile rather hard but apart from that, I should say that for most people morality is a web of beliefs rather than a number of unconnected ones." Devlin, *The Enforcement of Morals,* p. 115.

5. Devlin, *The Enforcement of Morality,* p. 13–14.

6. Hart, *Law, Liberty, and Morality*, p. 51.

7. Devlin, *The Enforcement of Morality*, pp. 115ff.

8. Devlin, *The Enforcement of Morality*, p. 116.

9. John Stuart Mill, *On Liberty* (New York: Liberal Arts Press, 1956), pp. 33–34.

10. James Fitzjames Stephen, *Liberty, Equality, Fraternity* (London: 1873), p. 163.

11. Cf. C. D. Broad, "Certain Features in Moore's Ethical Doctrines," in P. A. Schilpp, *The Philosophy of G. E. Moore* (Evanston, Ill.: Northwestern University Press, 1942), pp. 48 ff.

12. There have been some studies made, but the results have been inconclusive. See the *Report of the Federal Commission on Obscenity and Pornography* (New York: Bantam Books, 1970), pp. 169–308.

13. *Obscenity and Censorship* (Pamphlet published by the American Civil Liberties Union, New York, March, 1963), p. 7.

14. *Obscenity and Censorship*, p. 4.

15. Schwartz, "Morals Offenses and the Penal Code," 680.

16. Helen Merrill Lynd, *On Shame and the Search for Identity* (New York: Science Editions, Inc., 1961), p. 33.

17. Lynd, *On Shame and the Search for Identity*, p. 32.

18. William L. Prosser, *Handbook of the Law of Torts* (St. Paul: West Publishing Co., 1955), p. 411.

Part Two

Civil Disobedience

On Civil Disobedience

Hugo Bedau

Since I have been unable to find a suitably detailed analysis of what civil disobedience is and of its role in turning dissent into resistance, I have decided to try to provide such an analysis myself. This has left me with some space, but not much, to examine the problem of justifying this form of resistance to government.

I

1. A dissenter performs an act of civil disobedience only if he acts *illegally;* i.e., if he violates some positive law, because of (one of) the laws, policies, or decisions of his government which he finds objectionable. Acts of protest directed at government, no matter how conscientious or effective, in which no law is violated (as is usually the case with a poster parade, voluntary boycott, or refusal to accept government employment), are not acts of civil disobedience.[1] Civil disobedience, after all, is not just done; it is committed. It is always the sort of thing that can send one to jail.

As with any disobedience, it seems possible to distinguish between positive acts, which are the doing of something proscribed by law (e.g., trespassing on government property), and negative acts, which are the

From *The Journal of Philosophy* 48, no. 21 (October 12, 1961): 653–665. Reprinted by permission of the publisher and the author.

refusal to do something prescribed by law (e.g., not taking cover when directed to do so during an air raid drill). It has been suggested[2] that acts of the latter sort are almost always likely to be justified, perhaps on the ground that the consequences of abstaining from obedience can seldom be so disruptive as those of committing active disobedience. I am not convinced of this. For instance, widespread refusal of draft calls for military service would have a far greater effect on any "defense" establishment than would widespread trespassing on military bases. Nor do I see how doing something illegal by not going out of one's way to do something in particular is any more likely to be justified than doing something illegal by going out of one's way to do something in particular.

It is also possible to distinguish between those acts of dissent which, though illegal according to the authorities at hand, are believed by the dissenter to be within his legal rights as defined by the "fundamental law" or constitution as interpreted by the highest courts of the land (e.g., prior to the recent Supreme Court decisions in the Wilkinson and Braden cases, the refusal to testify about one's political beliefs and associations when questioned by a Congressional committee, on the ground that the First Amendment protects silence on such matters), and those acts which are committed without any belief in their judicial vindication (e.g., helping an escaped slave to keep his freedom in a slave state in the period immediately following the Supreme Court's decision in the Dred Scott case). This distinction is of some interest because, in the former class of cases, the dissenter quite possibly does not think of himself as committing an act of civil disobedience at all. But it seems irrelevant that his dispute with the government takes the form of a dispute over the legitimacy of a certain policy or of the authority of a certain government agency. So long as the authority at hand may, as it must, be permitted to define at least provisionally what is legal or within the scope of its authority, defying it can qualify as civil disobedience. The government may, as a rule, decide to treat this class of cases more leniently than those where there cannot be any reasonable hope of judicial vindication, but that is another matter.

Since all civil disobedience involves illegal activity, it has usually been supposed[3] that such acts could not receive legal protection; i.e., that there could be a legal right of civil disobedience (or of any form of resistance to government). What has not been noticed is that, by extending a practice already in use, civil disobedience could be lawfully eliminated. The law has long managed to obviate much civil disobedience by clauses providing exemption for conscientious objectors. There is no logical reason why every law could not have a rider to the effect that anyone who violates it on conscientious grounds shall be exempt from prosecution and penalty. The way in which such a provision would tend to weaken habitual obedience of the law and thus create problems for the police and the courts is obvious. But the fact that no government is likely even to consider such a provision, human nature being what it is, does not show any purely logical defect in extending this sort of legal protection to civil disobedience.

2. There would clearly be something odd about a policeman's reporting that he had surprised several persons in the act of committing civil disobedience or about employing detectives to root out conspiracies to commit civil disobedience. For this would suggest, contrary to fact, that these illegal acts were an embarrassment to the dissenter and that he might wish them to be kept secret from the public and especially from the government. Usually, though not always, it is essential to the purpose of the dissenter that both the public and the government should know what he intends to do. At least, it is essential that the government know of his act if it is intended that the government shall change its policy because of the act. This is one reason why the authorities are customarily notified in advance of those intending to commit civil disobedience. More fundamental still is the fact that the dissenter views what he does as a civic act, an act that properly belongs to the public life of the community. This derives from the fact that he thinks of himself as acting to thwart some law, policy, etc., that deviates from the true purpose of government as he sees it. Thus, his act draws attention to something he thinks the whole community should be brought to consider, since the community has as much interest in the act as he does. For these reasons, civil disobedience is necessarily *public*.

3. Not every illegal act of public resistance to government, however, is an act of civil disobedience. Anytime the dissenter resists government by deliberately destroying property, endangering life and limb, inciting to riot (e.g., sabotage, assassination, street fighting), he has not committed *civil* disobedience. The pun on 'civil' is essential; only *nonviolent* acts thus can qualify.[4] By 'nonviolent act' one means, I take it, that the agent

does not try to accomplish his aim either by initiating or by threatening violence, that he does not respond with violence or violent resistance during the course of his disobedience, regardless of the provocation he may have, and thus that he is prepared to suffer without defense the indignities and brutalities that often greet his act. Even if the reaction to his act is a violent one, whether by the police or by a hostile public, I do not think this negates the civility of his act; it is not a logical consequence of anyone's attempt to act nonviolently that anyone else should respond with violence.

4. The typical act of civil disobedience is not only directed against the government because of some objectionable law, policy, or decision and not only undertaken in order to frustrate that law, etc., but also so designed that the act itself does frustrate that law, etc. If this were the rule, no act could qualify for the title of civil disobedience unless it was the sort of act that, if it were committed by everyone (or even by a large minority), would hamper and perhaps prevent the government from enforcing the law, etc., at issue.

Here we meet an important distinction. Some acts of civil disobedience intend to achieve this aim by directly violating the objectionable law (e.g., refusing to register for the military draft), whereas other acts, like Thoreau's, intend to achieve this aim by violating some other law and are thus aimed at the objectionable law only indirectly (e.g., withholding from payment that portion of one's income taxes used to support the "defense" establishment). Since there are severe limitations to the circumstances in which certain laws are open to direct resistance by anyone except those who administer them (e.g., no ordinary citizen is in a position to resist directly his government's decision to launch a nuclear missile strike or to execute a condemned prisoner), it is only by acts of indirect resistance that it is possible for everyone to commit civil disobedience because of any of his government's laws. On the other hand, an act often allows of no more than a remote connection to the objectionable law, with the result that it appears ineffective and absurd. Hence, the preference among dissenters of cool head and stout heart for direct resistance.

What I have called 'direct resistance' must not be confused with what is popularly called 'direct action'. Direct action is a special form of direct resistance, in which the dissenter uses his own body as the lever with which to pry loose the government's policy. Nonviolent direct action takes either of two forms: "nonviolent obstruction" and "nonviolent interjection."⁵ Since the former involves a kind of physical coercion, albeit passive (e.g., climbing onto construction equipment and sitting there), it raises problems for those who scruple at the least suggestion of physical force in the act of disobedience. Thus, it is nonviolent interjection that is generally recognized to constitute the paradigm of every aspect of civil disobedience. Perhaps the most striking example in recent years was the voyage of The Golden Rule in the spring of 1958 into the Central Pacific, to try to force the United States government to abandon its nuclear-weapons testing program or to deliberately expose several of its citizens to a probably fatal dosage of radioactive fallout, since the crew intended to sail the ship directly into the testing area.⁶ The fashion in which such an act, without involving any conceivable physical coercion on the government, might force it to change (or at least to reappraise) its policy, is quite plain.

There is difficulty, however, in treating such cases as definitive, because not all illegal nonviolent public resistance to government constitutes even token frustration of the objectionable law that occasions the resistance. There is a whole class of acts, undertaken in the name of civil disobedience, which, even if they were widely practiced, would in themselves constitute hardly more than a nuisance (e.g., trespassing at a nuclear-missile installation). These acts may well serve as public witness to the integrity of the dissenter's convictions and may well lead to the commission of other acts that will frustrate the objectionable law. But overrunning a missile site with trespassers who only trespass and refuse to cooperate in their own arrest cannot really interfere with the construction of a. single launching pad or with the launching of a single missile. Therefore, such acts are often just a harassment and, at least to the bystander, somewhat inane. I am inclined, therefore, to treat this class of cases almost as border-line, even though it is one of the most popular kinds of civil disobedience at the present time in Great Britain and the United States. Bertrand Russell has recently suggested,⁷ apparently with this class of cases in mind, that civil disobedience that aims at altering the government's policy should be viewed essentially as "propaganda" directed at an acquiescent and uninformed public. Now it may be that the dissenter can derive incomparable propaganda advantage from acts which are not themselves even a feeble frustration of the law, policy, etc., that occasions them and which, even if widely practiced, would not in themselves bring a reversal of the government's position. But, once again, the remoteness of the connection between the disobedient act and the objectionable law lays such acts open to the charge of ineffectiveness and absurdity. Since, however, it is an empirical and not a logical question how effective such acts might be, they certainly can qualify as acts of civil disobedience.

Even among those acts of the former class which, in virtue of their structure, aim at frustrating the government's enforcement of the objectionable law, not all are undertaken in the hope of replacing that law with a better one or merely in this hope alone. The dissenter may act in such a way that he can thwart the application of the objectionable law only to himself (e.g., refusal to register for the military draft). At the other extreme, nonviolent resistance could even be undertaken with the intention of collapsing an entire government, as it has been claimed[8] the Hungarians under Francis Deak did a century ago against Austria. This latter class of cases is also somewhat border-line. Acting with intent to collapse the government obviously involves disloyalty, possibly sedition, and an unwillingness on the dissenter's part to acknowledge allegiance to that government and thus to accept the legal consequences of his act, including trial and imprisonment. Normally, committing civil disobedience does not involve acting with disloyal, seditious, traitorous, or rebellious intent, or with intent to resist, even nonviolently, the legal consequences of the act.[9] I see no logical reason, however, why civil disobedience could not aim at what Thoreau called "peaceable revolution."[10]

It is also worth noticing at this point that the civil disobedient need not be an anarchist. Contrary to some opinions, the decision to resist nonviolently to a certain law does not logically presuppose or entail the belief that all laws (or all this government's laws) ought to be resisted, or that governments and police forces are unnecessary, or that it is a sufficient condition for justifiably resisting the government on any occasion that it sanctions a manifestly unjust law. It may be that civil disobedience tends to encourage anarchism, as the classic Utilitarians believed, because respect for law may be weakened in the public at large (not to mention among the dissenters) even by an isolated act of resistance. Since it is true that habitual respect for the law is needed to allow the enforcement of manifestly just and beneficial laws, the conscientious dissenter will hesitate to undertake any act that would undermine this habit. But if worry about cultivating this habit figures prominently in government chancelleries, why is it that we continue to have incidents where even "democratic" governments complacently murder, kidnap, incite to rebel, lie, and break their solemn promises?

5. Civil disobedience is, finally, a *conscientious* act. That is, the dissenter proposes to justify his disobedience by an appeal to the incompatability between his political circumstances and his moral convictions. Usually, this requires that he be convinced that it would be worse for everyone to suffer the consequences of the objectionable law than it would be for everyone to suffer the consequences of his (and, conceivably, of everyone else's) civil disobedience. This requirement is reminiscent of Utilitarianism and one of its later variants[11] in that what is involved is a weighing of consequences against one another. But it is different in that such weighing is regarded here not as providing the criterion of justifiable civil disobedience but only as a condition of its conscientiousness. For not every conscientious act is justified, i.e., the right thing for the agent to do. Conscientiousness also usually requires that the dissenter acknowledge that the law, no matter what it is, makes some claim on his obedience, no matter how readily this claim may be overridden by other claims. Only an anarchist could think that his resistance was conscientious when he knew that he had taken nothing into account to justify himself except the fact that by this law the government sanctioned manifest injustice.[12] Why anyone should think a law is objectionable enough to deserve his resistance and why he should think his resistance ought to be nonviolent are quite independent considerations; there are any number of reasons why he might come to such conclusions. So the conscientiousness of the decision seems to lie in the way it is reached rather than in the nature of the convictions used to reach it.

It is not even necessary that the law because of which the disobedience is committed effect substantial injustice, violate basic rights, suffocate liberty, or otherwise work to the public disadvantage, though some such claim is almost invariably put forward. Though it may be highly improbable, there is no logical reason why a United States citizen could not commit acts of civil disobedience because of racial desegregation in the public schools, the Fifth Amendment, or foreign economic aid. A government, after all, can be subjected to conscientious resistance on account of *any* of its laws, policies, or decisions; and if anyone can have the right to resist conscientiously whatever he chooses, everyone else can have an equal right. I am even doubtful whether a civil disobedient must justify his resistance by appeal to the belief that the government sanctions manifest injustice, etc. I do not see any contradiction in his having no interest in that issue and still believing that his act is justified. It is true that disobedience that is mainly and patently self-serving raises doubts about its conscientiousness. But it is not a *logical* truth that people are easily self-deceived about their own motives, especially for those of their acts which benefit themselves. About the only moral convictions, therefore, we can assume in advance that a civil disobedient must have are that it is better to suffer violence than to inflict it and that law and order are not lightly to be disturbed. But since even these convictions need obtain only *ceteris paribus* (one need not, after all, be a Gandhian *Satyagrahi*), this is not saying much. Any number of circumstances might arise to override them, and there are any number of other convictions one might have with which they could conflict. I can conclude only and somewhat lamely that probably no one holds moral convictions that would rule out civil disobedience for him in every conceivable situation.

6. Are there specifiable political circumstances in which civil disobedience rather than another form of resistance or rather than no resistance at all is so unexceptionably justified that these circumstances constitute, as it were, part of the necessary context of any such act? I am not sure. Whenever legal devices for redress of grievances or for orderly change of laws and government personnel do not exist at all (e.g., the predicament of the dissenter in a totalitarian state) or when these devices have been exhausted for the foreseeable future (e.g., the predicament of the segregationist since the Supreme Court decision in Brown vs. Board of Education) or when it would take so much time to pursue these remedies that the objectionable law would meanwhile take its effect (e.g., the predicament of the crew of The Golden Rule), some sort of direct resistance to government is likely to be contemplated by the aggrieved parties. One is almost bound to insist that whenever such legal devices still obtain and civil disobedience or any other form of resistance is nevertheless committed, either the dissenter is acting irresponsibly, or his politics are anarchical, or both.[13] But even if these

legal devices do not obtain, that fact alone does not ordinarily suffice to justify resistance[14] nor to determine whether it should be direct or indirect, violent or nonviolent.

7. In the light of the foregoing examination, I suggest the following definition: Anyone commits an act of civil disobedience if and only if he acts illegally, publicly, nonviolently, and conscientiously with the intent to frustrate (one of) the laws, policies, or decisions of his government.

II

8. The radical possibility arises that whenever one is confronted by a law, one ought to disobey it—partly, as H. A. Prichard once suggested, because "after all the mere receipt of an order backed up by a threat seems, if anything, to give rise to the duty of resisting rather than of obeying"[15] but mainly just because "the certification of something as legally valid is not conclusive of the question of obedience."[16] That is, for a man to know that he ought to obey a certain law, policy, or decision of his government it is not sufficient if all he knows (or believes) is that the law, etc. is legally valid. This must be so, since 'I ought to do x' cannot be deduced from 'There is a valid law that applies to me and prescribes the doing of x.' So anyone's obligation to obey any law is pretty clearly contingent on what the law happens to be. Seen from this point of view, the concern of classic philosophers, such as Locke, to establish a "right" of resistance to government is unnecessary (and, when one recalls how they invariably hedged this right with obstacles before anyone could be in circumstances to justify his exercise of that right, somewhat ironical as well). For if we take the view that legal obligation is radically contingent, there is no problem at all in answering the question, 'How can anyone ever have a right to disobey the law?' The answer is simply, 'Because no one ever ought to do something just because it is the law.' Surely, it is because it is so often easy to see and to approve of what a law is designed to accomplish and to agree that it does, more or less, succeed, that one tends to overlook the heavy burden morality places on a law before it yields any authority to the law to guide one's conduct.

9. The problem of justifying one's decision to resist government arises because it is not sufficient to plead either any special defect of the objectionable law or the conscientiousness of one's decision. It may seem that one could not have a better reason for refusing to do what one's government orders than that one conscientiously believes it to be wrong. At least, it has been argued,[17] one cannot do any better than this and so is blameless. But we hesitate to allow that a man can know that he ought not to accept a certain policy of his government if all he knows is that he has conscientious scruples against it. It is logically possible that his moral convictions are most unfortunate, so that we would like nothing better than for anyone with his principles to fail in what he thinks he ought to do. His predicament (which is ours, too, of course) is that he cannot support his convictions and his estimate of his circumstances by appeal to some more objective and thus more authoritative appraisal, without also surrendering the opportunity to direct his own conduct. But it does not follow from the fact that a man cannot do more than what he conscientiously thinks he ought to do that he ought to do whatever he thinks he ought to do. The force of saying, 'I ought to disobey this law' cannot be derived from 'obeying this law is inconsistent with my moral convictions.' To enable the deduction obviously requires begging the question. The most we can say is that one has a right to conscientious disobedience; we need not and we cannot always go on to say that conscientious disobedience is the right thing to do. But being able to say the latter, and not just the former, is surely the main aim of trying to justify an act of disobedience.

Thus, it is possible that a government is sometimes right in having its way against the will of those who conscientiously disobey. So we cannot say, as some have,[18] that a government ought never to force a man to obey a law against his conscience. Perhaps one comes to the contrary view from supposing that no one's conscience could really advise him to disobey except in the name of justice, basic rights, freedom, or the general welfare and all that could be at issue is the relatively unimportant question of whether he or the government is right about the availability of those benefits under the law in question, since no government worthy of the name would aim at anything other than these ends, and that, in those cases where he is mistaken, the harm involved in forcing his compliance is always greater than the harm of letting him disobey and take the legal consequences. This is a set of amiable but nevertheless false suppositions.

10. Thus, the insufficiency of a law for obedience (and of conscientious scruples for disobedience) forces one to look elsewhere if one is to specify a principle that would identify the sufficient and necessary conditions, applicable in all situations, under which one's obedience (or disobedience) is justified. Unfortunately, I do not see how any such principle could be produced, or that it would be of any use once it was available. Any principle that could do the job required, being a principle of conduct, would itself be open to the very kind of demurrers and controversy it was designed to settle. Second, there is no compelling reason for anyone to adopt any principle in advance of knowing exactly what it will require of him. Since the kind of principle at issue here is likely to be formulated in the chronically open-textured moral concepts of justice, rights, and the like, one cannot know. Thus, anyone who searches for such a principle or who thinks he has one in hand really only disguises from himself the fact that the only way he could use his principle is by tacitly deciding on each occasion either to interpret the principle so as to cover the situation he is in or to describe the situation so as to fit the principle. This is why "the philosopher can offer no general rules which will enable a man to decide whether obedience or disobedience is the right course in a given case."[19]

11. The difficulties brought forward in the previous two sections do not bear particularly on civil disobedience; they apply to any resistance to government. They signify nothing more and nothing less than the fact that this kind of political behavior is bound to be morally relevant conduct and thus subject to the characteristic potentialities and risks of such conduct.

The question naturally arises whether there is anything special to be said on behalf of civil disobedience which perhaps puts it in a more favorable light than any of its alternatives, viz., violent resistance, obedience under legal public protest, furtive disobedience, or silent acquiescence. Many people evidently think so at present, since they reject these other alternatives out of hand. The first they usually reject because, even if they did not scruple at violence, which they do, they apparently have decided that it would not be successful in persuading their government or their fellow citizens to reexamine the objectionable law. They have also reasoned that violence would tend to excuse violent countermeasures, thereby crushing their capacity to continue the resistance. The other alternatives they dismiss either as ineffective or as something to be pursued only out of diffidence or cowardice in the face of the genuine dangers that active resistance can bring on the head of the dissenter. Their course they explain thus: Events in which the government's laws, policies, decisions, etc., play a decisive role are so distressing that if not soon improved they will lead to disaster. Therefore, directly or indirectly, action must be taken which could be fairly widely practiced (or threatened) and which, if it were, would force the government to change its course. Since one has no path to the seats of authority or to the minds of one's countrymen other than open resistance and since the method of resistance must be consistent, as far as possible, with preserving respect for law and order, the only thing to do is to commit civil disobedience, and the sooner the better.

The major obstacle in the way of granting a privileged status to such acts is that such status would rest on a series of empirical facts whose factuality is still in doubt. Is it true that a government can be brought to reverse its policy through civil disobedience alone? If so, what sort of government and what sort of policies? If not, under what circumstances can civil disobedience be effective? What sort of civil disobedience in general has the most chance of success? Is it false that a relatively bloodless coup is always less effective than civil disobedience? If the availability to the general public of a fairly clear-cut alternative, complete with step-by-step implementation, is necessary to the success of civil disobedience, can this condition always be satisfied in time? Is it really possible to influence the foreign relations of one nation through civil disobedience when there are serious and widespread doubts in the government and the public at large whether the dissenter's politics are acceptable to the other nation? These are a few of the familiar empirical questions that must be raised, and it is not too much to say that there is still responsible disagreement on the answers. The only way to get answers is to conduct actual experiments in civil disobedience. But it is one thing to commit such acts in order to help behavioral scientists get on with their work and another to commit them as though this work had been completed.

There is a regrettable failure on the part of dissenting minorities and those whom government has victimized to explore those situations in which civil disobedience might have some chance of success. Direct nonviolent resistance can often be conducted without interfering with community functions that no sane man would disrupt if he could avoid it. Speaking for myself, I think that, in such cases, civil disobedience would vastly improve the quality of individual participation in public affairs and perhaps accelerate the painfully slow and uncertain advance in the concern of governments for the aspirations of mankind.

NOTES

1. It has been suggested that work stoppages in arms factories are an ideal form of civil disobedience. But unless quitting a "defense" job is illegal, this is impossible. See Alan Lovell, "Direct Action," *New Left Review,* no. 8 (March–April, 1961): 20. As for the special problems of conscientious disobedience of military orders, which I have totally ignored, see Guenter Lewy, "Superior Orders, Nuclear Warfare, and the Dictates of Conscience," *American Political Science Review,* 55 (March, 1961): 3–23.

2. A. C. Ewing, *The Individual, the State and World Government* (New York, 1947), p. 69. The terms 'negative' and 'positive' as used in the text are borrowed from Ewing.

3. See Ewing, *op. cit.,* p. 73, and David Spitz, "Democracy and the Problem of Civil Disobedience," *American Political Science Review,* 48 (June, 1954): 342. See also Franz Neumann, "On the Limits of Justifiable Disobedience," reprinted in his *The Democratic and the Authoritarian State* (Glencoe, 1958), p. 154; he refers to Article 947 of the Constitution of Hesse (1946), which provides for "the right and the duty" of "resistance to unconstitutionally exercised public authority."

4. Bentham is typical of the classic philosophers from Bacon to Mill, all of whom tend to ignore civil disobedience. His sole conception of "open disobedience" to government is of "forcible" resistance, as though 'open' meant something other than 'public'. See his *Fragment of Government* (1776), F. C. Montague, ed. (Oxford, 1931), pp. 147 f. Not even Thoreau, who seems to have coined the phrase 'civil disobedience', stressed its nonviolent character. The matter has become obvious only since the writings of Gandhi. See his *Nonviolent Resistance* (New York, [1951] 1961), pp. 3–4.

5. This distinction and terminology I have taken from Bradford Lyttle, *Essays on Nonviolent Action* (Chicago [1959]), pp. 30f.

6. See Albert Bigelow, *The Voyage of The Golden Rule* (New York, 1959).

7. See his "Civil Disobedience," *New Statesman,* 61 (Feb. 17, 1961): 245f.

8. Richard Gregg, *The Power of Nonviolence* (New York, 1944), pp. 19f.

9. Some of the views Irving Kristol and Robert Penn Warren express

in "On Civil Disobedience and the Algerian War," *Yale Review*, 50 (Spring, 1961): 470 and 477, respectively, are quite remarkable in implying the contrary.

10. "Civil Disobedience" (1849), *The Portable Thoreau*, Carl Bode, ed. (New York, 1947), p. 123.

11. See Bentham, *op. cit.*, pp. 211, 215, 220, 227, and Ernest Barker, *Principles of Social and Political Theory* (Oxford, 1951), p. 224.

12. Thus, when it is said that a bill of attainder provides its victim with a sufficient condition for having "the right to resist," I suppose one would want to introduce some further considerations to determine when and how the agent ought to exercise this right. See Neumann, *op. cit.*, p. 158.

13. Thus, I tend to agree with those who think that the absence of these legal devices is a necessary condition of any form of justifiable resistance. See Guenter Lewy, "Resistance to Tyranny," *Western Political Quarterly*, 13 (September, 1960): 585, 591f.

14. Probably it does, if the government in question professes "democratic" principles and if the civil disobedience is undertaken on behalf of policies implied by those principles. See Spitz, *op. cit.*, pp. 396f.

15. *Moral Obligation* (Oxford, 1949), p. 54.

16. H. L. A. Hart, *The Concept of Law* (Oxford, 1961), p. 206.

17. Richard Brandt, *Ethical Theory* (Englewood Cliffs, N.J., 1959), p. 291.

18. Ewing, *op. cit.*, p. 68, and also, it would appear, Spitz, *op. cit.*, p. 400.

19. Ewing, *op. cit.*, p. 73. See also Bentham, *op. cit.*, p. 215; Barker, *op. cit.*, pp. 224f.; and most recently, S. I. Benn and R. S. Peters, *Social Principles and the Democratic State* (London, 1959), pp. 70f.

The United States Faces Today A Serious Threat to Her Continued Existence as a Free People

Leon Jaworski

I devoted a good deal of time over a period of two years studying the crime problem and deliberating over it—seeking as much information as I could possibly gather and finally trying to arrive, along with my fellow Commissioners of the President's Crime Commission, at some feasible and sensible solution. Following the filing of our report and our recommendations, I have continued to interest myself in this subject because I am fully aware of its overall importance—its complexities and perplexities.

Now I find myself in the middle of this problem in an effort to serve the American Bar Association in its program this year [1967], which has for its main thrust the control and prevention of crime. Actually, I find that it was relatively simple to serve as a member of a Commission making findings and conclusions and recommendations but not so simple to serve as the Chairman of a group that seeks to implement the report.

I need not begin with the citing of statistics disclosing the alarming rise in the crime rate. I assume that you know how serious this problem is and that unless we find an answer to it, the peace and tranquility

Address delivered to the Philosophical Society of Texas, December 8, 1967. Published in the *Baylor Line* January-February, 1968): 14–18. Reprinted by permission of the publisher.

that we have enjoyed within our own borders is gravely in danger of being lost. But I do think that we need to recall a few graphic illustrations of occurrences within our midst in recent months.

In one of our cities we find an officer of the law seeing a young man smash the window of a store to burglarize it. Rushing to the scene, the officer arrested him. Promptly a gathering took place. At first, 50 or 60 men surrounded the officer chanting, "Let him go." As the officer tried to put handcuffs on the suspect the officer was slugged from behind and pushed to the ground. The suspect broke free and ran. The officer drew his gun and caught the suspect after firing a warning shot in the air. At this point a crowd of 200 had gathered around the officer and began to menace him. Six husky members of the mob came toward the officer, one holding a sodawater bottle in his hand, saying, "We're going to take him away from you." The officer was hit on the hand with the bottle, and as the suspect broke free and fled, the mobsters moved in on the policeman who then was forced again to draw his gun to avoid their menacing approach. A man walked up behind the officer and said, "All right, officer, I'm with you." At that moment several patrol cars came rushing to the scene and the mob dispersed but not until the man who had come to the officer's aid was stabbed and fell to the ground.

In another of our cities an almost unbelievable incident occurred. A soldier was beaten and robbed aboard a subway train while some 25 passengers cheered his assailant. The soldier had just boarded the train when a man confronted him and said, "Give me your money or I'll kill you." When he refused, the man tore off his glasses and began beating him. Two detectives came into the car while the soldier was being assaulted and had to draw their guns on the crowd to achieve order. The detectives said, "We had no choice. They were all chanting— cheering on the assailant."

DISRESPECT FOR SYMBOL OF LAW

By no means is this conduct confined to other states. Not long ago in a neighboring city a gang of youngsters was engaged in acts of vandalism. An officer of the law undertook to interfere. Several of the youths charged him and assaulted him. He was saved from serious injury by other officers appearing on the scene, but not until these young gangsters had succeeded in beating him, then stomping his cap to demonstrate their disrespect for the symbol of law and order.

These illustrations we draw from the experiences of other people, and they can be multiplied many times. Yet, I am certain that we can call on our own experiences to demonstrate how serious conditions are. A few weeks ago after I arrived at my hotel in Washington, about 9:30 in the evening, I decided to take a walk. As I left the front of the hotel, the doorman, who knew me, asked me if I was intending to walk any distance. I replied that I hoped to walk a number of blocks; thereupon he cautioned me not to go more than two or three blocks from the hotel because of possible criminal violence. Two weeks after that I was in Chicago, at the University of Chicago Kellogg Center, and again about the same hour of the evening I chose to take a walk. The clerk at the desk cautioned me not to leave the campus, telling me to walk two or three blocks on either side of the Center but not beyond this point. Not many weeks ago an acquaintance of mine was taking a stroll in the River Oaks section of Houston where I live. It had just turned dark when he was assaulted by three men who robbed him and in the process, cut and injured him. Thugs and marauders take over our streets when darkness falls and even our homes are not secure at times.

This is what I want to discuss with you—crime and violence, disrespect for the law, disobedience and all of the other concomitants that make for conditions that bring about a disorderly society.

There may be disagreements on what spawned this avalanche of lawlessness. At times I fear that we are inclined to place the causes away from our own doorstep and at our neighbor's.

CITIZENS FLOUT LAWS THEY DISLIKE

Let us pause to examine our attitude toward law enforcement in actual practice. When we are called on to serve on a grand jury or a petit jury in criminal cases, are we ready to respond and make the sacrifices this public service entails or do we prefer to let others do it? When we know of law violations, are we prepared to appear as witnesses—or do we duck this public service because it takes time? When officials defy court orders, are we prepared to support the courts or do we approbate this flouting of the law because the defiance is in accord with our prejudices? When law enforcement officers are faced with crime problems and need the help of the good citizens, do we give them our support or do they get a deaf ear because we don't want to get "mixed up" in enforcement problems? What contribution are we willing to make to helping our youths pursue a life of good citizenship instead of stumbling into the pitfalls of crime?

The conditions that exist today are not traceable, in my judgment, solely to sources such as poverty, racial discrimination, broken homes and similar social ills—although these appear to be contributing factors. True, this nation has been guilty of failures of one kind and another from which we should expect to reap some disorder. But the main cause, in my opinion, is to be found in our attitude as a nation—an attitude that no longer embraces the virtue of a high regard for law.

Listen to the admonition of an illustrious Texan, Governor James Stephen Hogg, who died in 1890, after a distinguished record as Attorney General and in seeking the nomination for Governor, said:

> . . . I take this occasion to express my fealty to the law. Neither sentiment, personal taste nor political principles control my convictions in this respect. When laws are passed they should be enforced, for they are but the commands of the people to their officers. Idle and obnoxious ones should be repealed, but none of them can be disregarded except at the expense of official integrity. A people who would encourage and not condemn the crime of official delinquency have but to wait to glean oppression's harvest. *A government that permits a law disobeyed, commits itself to a precedent that in time will be pleaded in justification of anarchy.*

How prophetic are these words of caution! Have not some leaders of government in our nation been guilty of disregarding laws? Have not some of them been guilty of official delinquency in permitting— yes even encouraging—laws to be disobeyed? Have they not reaped the harvest of which Governor Hogg spoke?

A great theologian and lecturer, one of the most dynamic preachers of this age, Dr. John R. Sizoo, not long before his passing, said: "Disorder in human society always comes in one or two ways: either by breaking law or disregarding law, *and the second is always the worse of the two.* A civilization goes on the skids when principles which have brought it into being cease to be relevant."

CHOOSING LAWS TO OBEY, DANGEROUS

One of the most appalling and frightening of the trends in recent years is the self-serving practice of choosing which laws or court orders to obey and which to defy. The preachments that generate this attitude are cancerously dangerous to our system of government under law. To rest upon or hide behind the claim that if one's conscience speaks to the contrary, justification exists for ignoring laws or decrees is but to say that the rule of law is not to be the governing yardstick of our society's conduct.

If this philosophy is to be adopted, where are we? If the civil rights leader, for example, in "good conscience" disobeys a law or court decree because it offends his moral belief of what is right, then why should not his antagonist also be free to exercise this prerogative? And if both integrationists and segregationists, as these designations are commonly used, are to be exempt from obedience of laws on conscientious grounds, why should not the exemption extend to the bookie in Texas who in his heart can see no moral wrong in the placing of bets on horse-racing or to the tavern operator in our state whose conscientious beliefs lead him to no moral differentiation between the sale of whiskey by the drink and the sale of a fifth by the liquor store. The conscientious objector to the income tax may find this philosophy quite appealing. This line of reasoning can be extended ad infinitum and to major crimes as well. It is not difficult to foresee that under a system where one's beliefs are to be the test, killings now considered murder, would be viewed as justifiable homicide.

DESTROYS MORAL CONCERN

The inevitable result, whether this attitude be confined to violations of injunctions or to misdemeanors or felonies now on our statute books, is to weaken the foundation on which our system of law and order rests. It goes beyond such weakening, in fact, for it tends to destroy our moral concern for what we now consider wrong and evil. For if one type of law involving conduct now considered to be wicked is to be violated with indifference and impunity, soon another law prohibiting acts now considered to be evil will fall victim to this practice. A moral callousness to the preservation of what we now consider to be right and decent, reminiscent of the days of the fall of the Roman Empire, may well follow. Let us not forget the lines of wisdom of the poet, Alexander Pope:

> Vice is a monster of so frightful mien
> As, to be hated, needs but to be seen;
> Yet seen too oft, familiar with her face,
> We first endure, then pity, then embrace.

Common disrespect of some orders of our courts is sure to breed an attitude of disrespect for other laws, and if law after law is to wither on the vine of disrespect, society is destined to retrograde to the law of the jungle. If we disagree with an existing law, we have open to us the legislative processes to abolish it. If we disagree with a court order, we have the right of appeal; and if it is finally upheld, we as good Americans are obliged to respect it so long as it remains the law.

What are we to expect of our young boys and girls when they hear Governors shout their defiance of court orders? What are we to expect of our young boys and girls when they hear a Nobel Prize winner defy a court decree because, according to him, it does not agree with his conscience?

I am not unmindful of the need that exists to correct conditions that may be the roots of crime. But the streets and the highways and the campuses and the beaches are not the places for recourse. Under our constitutional form of government, recourse must be sought in the legislative halls and by due process of law.

Recently we witnessed the sad spectacle of teachers going on strike in New York and after an injunction was granted, finding these teachers disobeying the injunction. What a horrible example this sets for the students! To make matters worse, the leaders of this teacher group were hailed before the courts, charged with violating the law because of their refusal to obey the injunction, then sentenced for contempt of court. I can conceive of nothing that brings about a greater disrespect for law than the example these teachers set for their students.

NEW AND OLD ORDERS *CANNOT* CO-EXIST

Do we want a society regulated by law? The new order, espoused by some groups, termed "civil disobedience" and the old order, which meant respect for law, are incongruous. They cannot co-exist. If civil disobedience, as it has been practiced today, is to be commonly accepted, the rule of law will disappear. Which are we to choose?

It was the Roman Catholic Archbishop of Boston, Richard Cardinal Cushing, who in commenting on our cherished principles said: "Among these, is the principle that observance of law is the eternal safeguard of liberty, and defiance of law is the surest road to tyranny . . . even among law-abiding men, few laws are loved, but they are uniformly respected and not resisted."

Indeed, the doctrine of civil disobedience as generally practiced today is nothing but a trend toward organized lawlessness and rebellion.

LAW MEANINGLESS IF NOT SAME FOR ALL

"Where law ends, tyranny begins." These are the words of William Pitt. They are as true today as when he uttered them. When the courageous Judge of the New York State Supreme Court handed down a fifteen day jail sentence on the AFL-CIO United Federation of Teachers' strike leader, Albert Shanker, he declared: "Our existence as a free people is dependent on a healthy respect for law and order." Then he added, "Law means nothing unless it means the same law for all."

In the United States Supreme Court case convicting Martin Luther King and others of violating a court injunction it was said, ". . . No man can be judge in his own case, however exalted his station, however righteous his motives, and irrespective of his race, color, politics, or religion. . . . One may sympathize with the petitioners' impatient commitment to their cause. But respect for judicial process is a small price to pay for the civilizing hand of law, which alone can give abiding meaning to constitutional freedom."

SUPREME COURT RULINGS QUESTIONED

Some of us on the President's Crime Commission view with deep concern the effect of recent Supreme Court rulings, particularly the Miranda decision, setting out guidelines for the interrogation of suspects of crime. The majority on the Crime Commission chose not to comment on this subject, so those of us who felt strongly that the public should know the full impact of this decision on law enforcement concluded to file an addendum which appears at the end of the general report of the Crime Commission. Our fellow-member, Dean Robert Storey, and two other past Presidents of the American Bar Association and I joined in an addendum on this subject. After we prepared this separate statement, three other Commission members joined us in its presentation. Since its publication, another member of the Commission has given it full approval.

We raised the question whether some of the so-called guidelines set out by the Court do not result in seriously affecting the delicate balance between the rights of the individual and those of society. We raised the question of whether the scales have tilted in favor of the accused and against law enforcement and the public further than the best interest of the country permits.

Needless to say, we support these decisions as well as all decisions of the Supreme Court as the law of the land, to be respected and enforced unless and until changed by the processes available under our form of government. But these constitutional limitations, in our judgment, have an adverse effect upon law enforcement agencies and we thought that the public should be fully aware of these conclusions. If the adverse effect is serious enough, remedial action should be considered. A Senate Committee is concerning itself with the problem now.

It has been pointed out that these decisions do not increase crime. Without conceding the point, in my view, these decisions do affect the efficacy of law enforcement. I further believe that when the effectiveness of law enforcement is diminished it not only affects the morale of the peace officer—it also is discouraging to the citizen who believes in a policy of strict law enforcement.

NATION FACES GRAVEST CRIME PROBLEM IN HISTORY

Considerable of the Commission's work was devoted to the awesome problem of juvenile delinquency. Of persons arrested for serious crimes last year, nearly one-half were youngsters under eighteen years of age. The Crime Commission found that generally a juvenile record is a forerunner of adult crime. It found that "the earlier a child is arrested for some offense, the more likely it is that he will become an adult offender in the years ahead." It is not difficult to foresee that in the light of the striking increase of youth crime our nation is confronted with a crime problem far graver than anything it has faced before.

What needs to be done? I have no panacea—but this much I think we can agree upon: resorting to legislating alone, pontificating, "cursing the darkness" and similar acts and emotions do not give us the answer. Rather, it will take a dedicated and determined lawful uprising against crime—with the good citizens of our country setting the example in total support of law and order. It will require a militancy that begins at home, permeates the educational institutions, challenges civic organizations and religious institutions into action and continues in revolt until the ugly face of crime has been changed.

A SOLUTION THAT WORKED

A few years ago, the country of Brazil was on the brink of falling into the hands of Communists. One Government decree after another robbed the people of Brazil of their freedoms and their possessions. Sensing the danger, hundreds of housewives rushed to their telephones to begin organizing a demonstration. Six days later, on March 19, the wide thoroughfares of downtown Sao Paulo were jammed with what the women called the "March of the Family With God Toward Freedom." Clutching prayerbooks and rosaries, a vast army more than 600,000 strong marched in solemn rhythm under anti-communist banners. And as they marched, newshawks on the sidelines sold newspapers containing a 1,300 word proclamation the women had prepared. It read in part:

> This nation which God has given us, immense and marvelous as it is, is in extreme danger. We have allowed men of limitless ambition, without

Christian faith or scruples, to bring our people misery, destroying our economy, disturbing our social peace, to create hate and despair. They have infiltrated our nation, our government administration, our armed forces and even our churches with servants of totalitarianism, foreign to us and all-consuming. . . . Mother of God, preserve us from the fate and suffering of the martyred women of Cuba, Poland, Hungary, and other enslaved nations!

One bystander called the Sao Paulo women's march "the most moving demonstration in Brazilian history." Days later, similar marches were scheduled for several of that nation's major cities. Efforts by the government to discourage them, and threats by police to break them up, failed to halt the crusading women.

This action on the part of the women of Brazil, more than anything else, saved that nation from falling into the hands of the Communists. It is a stirring illustration of what a determined people can do.

HISTORY WILL RECORD ANSWER

Will there be a militant citizen's movement to bring about a new and different attitude towards crime in our country or will we let matters retrogress to an even worse state than exists today? You and I, and other citizens across the land, have a part in writing the answer—and history will record it.

Disobedience as a Psychological and Moral Problem

Erich Fromm

For centuries kings, priests, feudal lords, industrial bosses and parents have insisted that *obedience is a virtue* and that *disobedience is a vice.* In order to introduce another point of view, let us set against this position the following statement: *human history began with an act of disobedience, and it is not unlikely that it will be terminated by an act of obedience.*

Human history was ushered in by an act of disobedience according to the Hebrew and Greek myths. Adam and Eve, living in the Garden of Eden, were part of nature; they were in harmony with it, yet did not transcend it. They were in nature as the fetus is in the womb of the mother. They were human, and at the same time not yet human. All this changed when they disobeyed an order. By breaking the ties with earth and mother, by cutting the umbilical cord, man emerged from a pre-human harmony and was able to take the first step into independence and freedom. The act of disobedience set Adam and Eve free and opened their eyes. They recognized each other as strangers and the world outside them as strange and even hostile. Their act of disobedience broke the primary bond with nature and made them individuals. "Original sin," far from corrupting man, set him free; it was the beginning of history. Man had to leave the Garden of Eden in order to learn to rely on his own powers and to become fully human.

The prophets, in their messianic concept, confirmed the idea that man had been right in disobeying; that he had not been corrupted by his "sin," but freed from the fetters of pre-human harmony. For the prophets, *history* is the place where man becomes human; during its unfolding he develops his powers of reason and of love until he creates a new harmony between himself, his fellow man and nature. This new harmony is described as "the end of days," that period of history in which there is peace between man and man, and between man and nature. It is a "new" paradise created by man himself, and one which he alone could create because he was forced to leave the "old" paradise as a result of his disobedience.

Just as the Hebrew myth of Adam and Eve, so the Greek myth of Prometheus sees all of human civilization based on an act of dis-obedience. Prometheus, in stealing the fire from the gods, lays the foundation for the evolution of man. There would be no human history were it not for Prometheus' "crime." He, like Adam and Eve, is punished for his disobedience. But he does not repent and ask for forgiveness. On the contrary, he proudly says: "I would rather be chained to this rock than be the obedient servant of the gods."

Man has continued to evolve by acts of disobedience. Not only was his spiritual development possible only because there were men who dared to say no to the powers that be in the name of their conscience or their faith, but also his intellectual development was dependent on the capacity for being disobedient—disobedient to authorities who tried to muzzle new thoughts and to the authority of long-established opinions which declared a change to be nonsense.

If the capacity for disobedience constituted the beginning of human history, obedience might very well, as I have said, cause the end of human history. I am not speaking symbolically or poetically. There is the possibility, or even the probability, that the human race will destroy civilization and even all life upon earth within the next five to ten years. There is no rationality or sense in it. But the fact is that, while we are living technically in the Atomic Age, the majority of men—including most of those who are in power—still live emotionally in the Stone Age; that while our mathematics, astronomy, and the natural sciences are of the twentieth century, most of our ideas about politics, the state, and society lag far behind the age of science. If mankind commits suicide it will be because people will obey those who command them to push the deadly buttons; because they will obey the archaic passions of fear, hate, and greed; because they will obey obsolete clichés of State sovereignty and national honor. The Soviet leaders talk much about revolutions, and we in the "free world" talk much about freedom. Yet they and we discourage disobedience—in the Soviet Union explicitly and by force, in the free world implicitly and by the more subtle methods of persuasion.

But I do not mean to say that all disobedience is a virtue and all obedience a vice. Such a view would ignore the dialectical relationship between obedience and disobedience. Whenever the principles which are obeyed and those which are disobeyed are irreconcilable, an act of obedience to one principle is necessarily an act of disobedience to its counterpart, and vice versa. Antigone is the classic example of this dichotomy. By obeying the inhuman laws of the State, Antigone necessarily would disobey the laws of humanity. By obeying the latter, she must disobey the former. All martyrs of religious faiths, of freedom and of science have had to disobey those who wanted to muzzle them in order to obey their own consciences, the laws of humanity and of reason. If a man can only obey and not disobey, he is a slave; if he can only disobey and not obey, he is a rebel (not a revolutionary); he acts out of anger, disappointment, resentment, yet not in the name of a conviction or a principle.

However, in order to prevent a confusion of terms an important qualification must be made. Obedience to a person, institution or power (heteronomous obedience) is submission; it implies the abdication of my autonomy and the acceptance of a foreign will or judgment in place of my own. Obedience to my own reason or conviction (autonomous obedience) is not an act of submission but one of affirmation. My conviction and my judgment, if authentically mine, are part of me. If I follow them rather than the judgment of others, I am being myself; hence the word *obey* can be applied only in a metaphorical sense and with a meaning which is fundamentally different from the one in the case of "heteronomous obedience."

But this distinction still needs two further qualifications, one with regard to the concept of conscience and the other with regard to the concept of authority.

The word *conscience* is used to express two phenomena which are quite distinct from each other. One is the "authoritarian conscience" which is the internalized voice of an authority whom we are eager to please and afraid of displeasing. This authoritarian conscience is what most people experience when they obey their conscience. It is also the conscience which Freud speaks of, and which he called "Super-Ego." This Super-Ego represents the internalized commands and prohibitions of father, accepted by the son out of fear. Different from the authoritarian conscience is the "humanistic conscience"; this is the voice present in every human being and independent from external sanctions and rewards. Humanistic conscience is based on the fact that as human beings we have an intuitive knowledge of what is human and inhuman, what is conducive of life and what is destructive of life. This conscience serves our functioning as human beings. It is the voice which calls us back to ourselves, to our humanity.

Authoritarian conscience (Super-Ego) is still obedience to a power outside of myself, even though this power has been internalized. Consciously I believe that I am following *my* conscience; in effect, however, I have swallowed the principles of *power*; just because of the illusion that humanistic conscience and Super-Ego are identical, internalized authority is so much more effective than the authority which is clearly experienced as not being part of me. Obedience to the "authoritarian conscience," like all obedience to outside thoughts and power, tends to debilitate "humanistic conscience," the ability to be and to judge oneself.

The statement, on the other hand, that obedience to another person is *ipso facto* submission needs also to be qualified by distinguishing "irrational" from "rational" authority. An example of rational authority is to be found in the relationship between student and teacher; one of irrational authority in the relationship between slave and master. Both relationships are based on the fact that the authority of the person in command is accepted. Dynamically, however, they are of a different nature. The interests of the teacher and the student, in the ideal case, lie in the same direction. The teacher is satisfied if he succeeds in furthering the student; if he has failed to do so, the failure is his and the student's. The slave owner, on the other hand, wants to exploit the slave as much as possible. The more he gets out of him the more satisfied he is. At the same time, the slave tries to defend as best he can his claims for a minimum of happiness. The interests of slave and master are antagonistic, because what is advantageous to the one is detrimental to the other. The superiority of the one over the other has a different function in each case; in the first it is the condition for the furtherance of the person subjected to the authority, and in the second it is the condition for his exploitation. Another distinction runs parallel to this: rational authority is rational because the authority, whether it is held by a teacher or a captain of a ship giving orders in an emergency, acts in the name of reason which, being universal, I can accept without submitting. Irrational authority has to use force or suggestion, because no one would let himself be exploited if he were free to prevent it.

Why is man so prone to obey and why is it so difficult for him to disobey? As long as I am obedient to the power of the State, the Church, or public opinion, I feel safe and protected. In fact it makes little difference what power it is that I am obedient to. It is always an institution, or men, who use force in one form or another and who fraudulently claim omniscience and omnipotence. My obedience makes me part of the power I worship, and hence I feel strong. I can make no error, since it decides for me; I cannot be alone, because it watches over me; I cannot commit a sin, because it does not let me do so, and even if I do sin, the punishment is only the way of returning to the almighty power.

In order to disobey, one must have the courage to be alone, to err and to sin. But courage is not enough. The capacity for courage depends on a person's state of development. Only if a person has emerged from mother's lap and father's commands, only if he has emerged as a fully developed individual and thus has acquired the capacity to think and feel for himself, only then can he have the courage to say "no" to power, to disobey.

A person can become free through acts of disobedience by learning to say no to power. But not only is the capacity for disobedience the condition for freedom; freedom is also the condition for disobedience. If I am afraid of freedom, I cannot dare to say "no," I cannot have the courage to be disobedient. Indeed, freedom and the capacity for disobedience are inseparable; hence any social, political, and religious system which proclaims freedom, yet stamps out disobedience, cannot speak the truth.

There is another reason why it is so difficult to dare to disobey, to say "no" to power. During most of human history obedience has been identified with virtue and disobedience with sin. The reason is simple: thus far throughout most of history a minority has ruled over the majority. This rule was made necessary by the fact that there was only enough of the good things of life for the few, and only the crumbs remained for the many. If the few wanted to enjoy the good things and, beyond that, to have the many serve them and work for them, one condition was necessary: the many had to learn obedience. To be sure, obedience can be established by sheer force. But this method has many disadvantages. It constitutes a constant threat that one day the many might have the means to overthrow the few by force; furthermore there are many kinds of work which cannot be done properly if nothing but fear is behind the obedience. Hence the obedience which is only rooted in the fear of force must be transformed into one rooted in man's heart. Man must want and even need to obey, instead of only fearing to disobey. If this is to be achieved, power must assume the qualities of the All Good, of the All Wise; it must become All Knowing. If this happens, power can proclaim that disobedience is sin and obedience virtue; and once this has been proclaimed, the many can accept obedience because it is good and detest disobedience because it is bad, rather than to detest themselves for being cowards. From Luther to the nineteenth century one was concerned with overt and explicit authorities. Luther, the pope, the princes, wanted to uphold it; the middle class, the workers, the philosophers, tried to uproot it. The fight against authority in the State as well as in the family was often the very basis for the development of an independent and daring person. The fight against authority was inseparable from the intellectual mood which characterized the philosophers of the enlightenment and the scientists. This "critical mood" was one of faith in reason, and at the same time of doubt in everything which is said or thought, inasmuch as it is based on tradition, superstition, custom, power. The principles *sapere aude* and *de omnibus est dubitandum*—"dare to be wise" and "of all one must doubt"—were characteristic of the attitude which permitted and furthered the capacity to say "no."

The case of Adolf Eichmann is symbolic of our situation and has a significance far beyond the one which his accusers in the courtroom in Jerusalem were concerned with. Eichmann is a symbol of the organization man, of the alienated bureaucrat for whom men, women and children have become numbers. He is a symbol of all of us. We can see ourselves in Eichmann. But the most frightening thing about him is that after the entire story was told in terms of his own admissions, he was able in perfect good faith to plead his innocence. It is clear that if he were once more in the same situation he would do it again. And so would we—and so do we.

The organization man has lost the capacity to disobey, he is not even aware of the fact that he obeys. At this point in history the capacity to doubt, to criticize and to disobey may be all that stands between a future for mankind and the end of civilization.

Justifying Civil Disobedience

Rudolph H. Weingartner*

I

In general, we ought to obey the law. Suppose I ask whether I should do *A* or *B*; if you then tell me that to do *A* is to break the law, surely this information must weigh on the side of *B* and count against *A*. It is not a conclusive reason for not doing *A*, for, as I shall suggest, the arguments designed to show that breaking the law is never justified are not successful. What the truth of this generalization does show, however, is that any breach of the law is in *need* of a justification, that it is not one of those matters—like telling the truth or being kind to children—that requires justification only under special circumstances.

This may be obvious in most cases of lawbreaking, but it seems not to be so obvious when it comes to civil disobedience. Indeed, so much passion has of late been aroused by the issue of civil disobedience that we are scarcely aware of the lack of clarity in our thinking about

From *Columbia Forum* 9 (Spring, 1966). Reprinted by permission of the publisher and the author.

*I have learned much from the following: Hugo A. Bedau, "On Civil Disobedience," *Journal of Philosophy,* 58 (1961); Charles L. Black, Jr., "The Problem of the Compatibility of Civil Disobedience with American Institutions of Government," *Texas Law Review,* 43 (1965); Carl Cohen, "Essence and Ethics of Civil Disobedience," *The Nation,* 198 (1964); John Dickinson, "A Working Theory of Sovereignty II," *Political Science Quarterly,* 43 (1928); Morris Keeton, "The Morality of Civil Disobedience," *Texas Law Review,* 43 (1965); Harold Laski, *The State in Theory and Practice,* New York, 1935; Richard A. Wasserstrom, "The Obligation to Obey the Law," *UCLA Law Review,* 10 (1963).

the subject. More than one commentator discussing the rioting and violence in the Watts district of Los Angeles in the summer of 1965 used the term "civil disobedience" in referring to events and actions to which it certainly does not apply. Before discussing its justification, it would be well to consider what civil disobedience is.

Civil disobedience is, above all, disobedience. It is the violation of a command issued by an authority, such as a government, that has a claim to our obedience. When a number of people disobey a bank official who asks them to leave the bank and to cease immobilizing it by perpetually requesting coins to be changed into bills and bills into coins, it is not civil disobedience, unless a law is also broken. The law has a claim to our obedience; bank officials as such do not. Where a government is not directly confronted in an illegal act, there may be a strike, a boycott, harassment, or some other kind of pressure, but not civil disobedience. Nor is *legal* non-obedience of the law civil disobedience. Conscientious objectors are exempted from service in the armed forces, and Jehovah's Witnesses are permitted to refrain from saluting the flag. Neither group is engaged in civil disobedience.

Moreover, civil disobedience must be *civil* disobedience of a law. If those who disobey the law use violence in doing so, they are no longer practicing civil disobedience. For while the violence may overtly be aimed at private persons, it is at least implicitly directed against those charged with enforcing the law. But to that extent the act is no longer confined to the transgression of a particular law; instead it becomes a defiance of the authority that makes and enforces the laws. Violent disobedience is not simply a noisier kind of civil disobedience; it is rebellion.

This distinction is an important one. Rebellion or revolution, whether it is peaceful or violent, aims to modify the established order either by supplanting those who make and enforce the laws, or by changing the very processes of legislation and enforcement, or by doing both. The change sought is not simply a change in one or another law, but of the entire framework within which laws are made and carried out. Accordingly, insofar as Gandhi aimed at the elimination of British rule in India, he was a revolutionary, for civil disobedience aims at a particular law or governmental measure, and not at the state itself. An important though not infallible symbol of this distinction is that in the clearest cases of civil disobedience those engaged in it are willing to accept the punishment that is meted out to those who break the law in question.

They use violence neither in disobeying the law nor in their reaction to arrest, trial, and the sentencing that may follow disobedience.

But surely, most people who disobey a law non-violently are not thereby practicing civil disobedience. A person may knowingly park in a no-parking zone hoping not to get caught and be ready, if not happy, to pay the fine if he is so unlucky as to be found out. Still, this does not make him a practitioner of civil disobedience. Whoever engages in civil disobedience commits an illegal act because he takes a law or governmental measure to be wrong; he seeks to protest and possibly to change a wrong done by the state, pitting what he takes to be right— that is to say moral—against what the state takes to be right—that is to say, at least legal. There is no type of law or governmental measure which is, by its nature, immune to civil disobedience; moreover, the *way* in which a law or measure might be found wanting must be left open. Some laws are protested because they are thought unjust; others because they are taken to transgress a divine commandment; some because they are thought to violate rights possessed by all men; still others because they are held to produce effects contrary to the common good. To say that the goal must be moral requires that the illegal act not be undertaken simply to gain an advantage for the actor. And because it is not always so clear what someone's purposes may be (including one's own), the willingness to accept punishment is a useful sign that the disobedience is not simply the means to a private end.

It does not follow from this that a Negro can never employ genuine civil disobedience in order to bring about civil rights for Negroes, or that his actions must be seen as self-seeking, however understandable—analogous, say, to a steelworker's strike for higher wages. A Negro practitioner of civil disobedience will undoubtedly be better off if he succeeds in bringing about a change in the laws. But the question of purposes is not settled by such a consideration of effects. If an illegal act is performed in order to protest against a law for being unjust or contrary to the good of the community, then it is civil disobedience, even if justice or the common good is also to the advantage of the protester. What remains of fundamental importance for the identification of an act of civil disobedience and for its justification alike is that the purposes of the act be moral.

Finally, the activity of civil disobedience must be public. Simple evasion of the law, even when undertaken for the highest reasons of conscience, is not yet civil disobedience. The physician, for example, who quietly administers a fatal injection to an incurable patient in order to relieve great suffering evades a law but does not engage in civil disobedience. Even if the doctor is resigned to accepting punishment should he be found out, his act is not civil disobedience unless he intends his transgression to be publicly known. Civil disobedience *usually* involves an unwillingness to obey a law thought to be wrong, but it *always* constitutes a protest against a law or governmental measure. And a protest is more than the expression of a disagreement; it includes a desire for change. As such, the evasion of a law makes no contribution to getting a law or policy revoked or modified. For an act of conscience to be also one of protest, it must at least potentially be able to persuade others. That the whole town knew of Thoreau's imprisonment was not adventitious: it was a part of his civil disobedience.

An act of civil disobedience, to sum up, is an illegal, non-violent, moral, and public protest against a law or governmental measure.

I want also to distinguish between two types of civil disobedience, *direct* and *indirect*, a difference that will have a bearing on the question of justification. In some cases of civil disobedience, the very law that is being protested against is the one disobeyed. It is direct civil disobedience when a law calls for the separate seating of whites and Negroes, and a person violates that very law because he thinks it is wrong. But in many instances, civil disobedience cannot take so straightforward a form. The suffragettes who fought for women's rights could not disobey the law that disenfranchised them. These militant ladies violated trespassing laws, statutes against disturbing the peace, and the like.

Clearly, indirect civil disobedience is the only kind that is possible when the wrong being protested is the *absence* of a law or a governmental measure. But often, too, indirect civil disobedience is the only possible form of disobedience when the protest is directed against a law or measure that *does* exist. The ordinary citizen, for example, cannot readily interfere with the testing of nuclear arms or the appropriation of money for war, so that the law or command to be disobeyed will have to be different from that being protested against. The connection between the object of protest and the measure violated may be close: the suffragettes disturbed the peace at political meetings of campaigners who did not support the proposal to give women the vote. At other times there is no intrinsic connection at all: Bertrand Russell was arrested for refusing to keep the peace as a protest against nuclear arms.

II

Society requires order for its existence. Throughout history this need has been affirmed with passion and pursued with singlemindedness. It is thus not surprising that many men have held that one is never justified in breaking a law and that civil disobedience is always wrong. On the other hand, in more than one reformation has the conscience of the individual been raised above the rules of institutions and the mores of society. Accordingly, we have been urged never to obey a law that we think is wrong. In this view civil disobedience is then always justified when directed against laws that conflict with one's convictions. I think both of these views are wrong and I shall furthermore argue that there cannot even be a general rule which serves to decide when civil disobedience is justified and when it is not.

Some have claimed that it is never morally right to disobey the law because morality simply consists in obedience to the laws. This is an ancient doctrine that tries to define what is right wholly in terms of what the laws say is right. And its reputation is equally old. Laws conflict at least from one period to another and from place to place; if rightness were constituted by what the laws dictate, then we are led to the weird conclusion that the same act can be both right and not right, or, whenever the law is silent, be neither right nor not right. Moreover, this logical identification of morality with law would make it meaningless nonsense to evaluate a law: to censure a law as unjust or to praise it as in accord with morality would have to be considered as unintelligible as criticizing squares for having right angles or praising them for having sides that are straight.

Then, it has been held that any law which fails to conform to the demands of morality is not truly a law. But surely this is an odd view of the nature of laws. It makes well-nigh irrelevant to their characters as laws their creation and promulgation by a properly constituted legislature, their enforcement by a legitimate executive, and their application by an acknowledged judiciary. To define the legal in terms of the moral makes little more sense than to define the moral in terms of the legal.

Others have granted that morality and legality can and do diverge, but they nevertheless hold that one is never justified in disobeying a law, because of the difficulties of *determining* what is right. Their argument may be formulated in this way:

Societies differ greatly in the ways in which their laws are made. The law of the land may be the word of a single, unquestioned sovereign, or the product of assemblies in which all the people participate. Secular authorities create and interpret the laws in some societies; in others, a special priestly class reads the will of the gods. But no group of men that is rightly called a society is without a relatively stable method for answering the question, what does the law say with regard to this matter? It may be a difficult one to answer, but at least it is always possible to point to some social institutions whose job it is to answer it, and to standards, however crude, by which the adequacy of any answer can be measured.

The moral realm is not similarly favored. Individuals and groups, some more powerful than others, all have opinions as to what is right. While there may be much agreement, there is also conflict. Above all, there is no recognized authority to adjudicate moral disputes. No doubt, it is then argued, there are differences between what is right and what is legal, but there is no institution that determines whether what someone thinks to be wrong actually *is* wrong. Accordingly, no one is ever justified in disobeying a law on the grounds that the law is wrong, for who can say what is right?

Two replies can be made to this objection to civil disobedience. First, the lack of an institution for making moral decisions does not imply that there cannot be reasons—even conclusive reasons—in support of a moral claim. Whatever may be the conditions for definitiveness in moral judgment, the existence of special institutions is surely not a necessary one, however, much their existence may help in securing agreement. And agreement is precisely what should not be expected. More often than not, the moral critic of the law proposes to apply to the law a higher, a finer, or a more advanced standard of morality than do the institutions that make and interpret the laws. In a democracy at least, these legal institutions can be expected to be quite close to the moral norm of the community, so that the critic is not likely to find pervasive assent to his views.

Second, the lack of an institution for determining what is right is not sufficient ground for failing to do what one thinks is right. For there is never an institution that dispenses the correct answer and secures everyone's agreement to boot. While not everything we do is as grave as civil disobedience, some acts we perform, such as begetting children or going off to war—acts that do not conflict with the law—are at least of equal gravity. Yet neither the lack of a sure method of decision nor the absence of agreement should or does stop us from acting. What one thinks is right does not always turn out to be so, but it would be strange advice never to do what one thinks is right simply because others do not agree or because one *might* be wrong.

This leads to a final group of arguments in support of the thesis that civil disobedience is never justified. These arguments claim, in various ways, that the social consequences of civil disobedience are always worse than those of obedience. "What if everybody did it?" is the question to which a fatal sting is attributed; and of course the prospect of a society in which no one obeys the law is frightening. But just what is the connection between one person's act of civil disobedience and the chaos of a lawless society? Surely it is evident that such an act does not actually bring about the commission of countless other breaches of law. Indeed, an act of civil disobedience may confirm more citizens in their legal rectitude than it induces to break laws. What causes what is a question of empirical fact, and observation simply fails to bear out the contention that *everyone* will do what *somebody* does. And if it is argued that the risk of violence, the suffering of punishment, and other such consequences of disobeying the law will always be worse than those of obedience to the law, I must reply that this is all too grandiose a claim about the way of the world. Whether the consequences of one act are better or worse than those of another is a matter of looking and seeing; to say that one type of act *must* be better than another, regardless of the circumstances, is not warranted by any general law about human behavior.

What now of the other side of the controversy? Have not the floodgates been opened to the view that whenever one thinks the law to be wrong, civil disobedience is justified? Laws ought to be obeyed, some have maintained, only when and if they are morally right. And who else but each person himself can judge the moral adequacy of the law? When he judges the law to be morally deficient, he is at least *justified* in disobeying it and possibly *obligated* to do so. It is even held that men who do not act on what they think is right give up their function as citizens; surely, it is argued, men give up their dignity as moral agents unless they themselves determine what they ought to do.

There is a nobility to this position which makes it an attractive one; nevertheless, I think that it is at best confused. First there is the matter of conscientiousness: I might take a law to be wrong on the basis of quick and superficial thought or I might come to this conclusion after prolonged reflection. I may be ignorant of the issues involved or I may have made a special study of them. The following sentence, accordingly, is not paradoxical, but merely expresses the complexity of moral judgments: "I think this law is morally wrong, but because you are more knowledgeable than I about its long-range effects, I concede that you may be right in saying that the law is good." If civil disobedience is justified when one thinks a law to be wrong, then surely it is justified only to the degree to which one is entitled to one's opinion.

Second, there is a vast difference between judging that a law is wrong and judging that one ought to disobey it. Even if I am correct in thinking that a particular law requires an act that is morally wrong (or the omission of one that is needed), it by no means just follows that I should disobey it. For many other considerations must enter into a decision to disobey a law, even after the question of the rightness of the law has been already settled. It is not self-contradictory to say that such and such a law is wrong, but that it ought to be obeyed. One is therefore not automatically justified in disobeying *any* law one thinks is wrong, much less in protesting publicly against it.

It has now been shown, I think, that the extreme positions on the justifiability of civil disobedience are difficult to maintain: civil disobedience is neither prohibited nor permitted by some perfectly general formula. Indeed, there is no simple way of dealing with the ethics of civil disobedience, for it can be demonstrated that there cannot even be a rule that serves to decide when civil disobedience is and when it is not justified.

Surely, one might contend, all those cases in which civil disobedience is justified share some characteristic, simple or complex, that the unjustifiable ones do not possess. And in a sense, this is indeed true. One may be justified in disobeying a law if, after one has conscientiously reflected on all the relevant factors, one has good evidence that a greater good is achieved by breaking than by obeying it. Correct or not, this rule is at least plausible; still it will not serve to decide when one is justified in breaking a law. How much reflection is conscientious reflection? Which factors are relevant factors? How much evidence is good evidence? And which goods are greater than which? These questions are not simple ones and for none is the answer the same for all possible cases. (What is good enough evidence for breaking a date need not be good enough for breaking the engagement.)

We could agree to accept such a rule and cease asking which cases of civil disobedience are justified. But in exchange we inherit the new problem of finding out to which cases the rule applies. The gain is only apparent: the simplicity of a wholesale solution is illusory.

III

We are now left with the requirement that each case of civil disobedience must be examined on its own merits. The best that we can do is to spell out what some of the relevant considerations are which help to decide whether or not a case of civil disobedience is justified. It will be convenient to discuss these issues under five general headings, though I have no illusions that the list is exhaustive.

1. *The wrongness of the law.* Civil disobedience is justified to the degree to which the object of the protest is thought to be wrong. If the law or measure is not thought to be wrong at all, breaking it does not constitute civil disobedience; if it is thought to be wrong only in a trivial or minor way, its wrongness cannot outweigh either the general obligation we have to obey the law or the disadvantageous consequences of civil disobedience. If the wrong is thought to be grievous, civil disobedience may be more readily justified.

Two comments. It is assumed here, as it is throughout this essay, that, in principle, questions of right and wrong have answers, even if in fact we often fail to arrive at them. Such a view of morals as objective, however, does not require us to suppose that there are simple moral absolutes holding for all times and places. Rather, to hold that criteria in ethics are objective and to say that moral questions have answers is to assert above all that what is right or wrong is conceptually independent of what happens to be thought right or wrong—by a few people or even by all. (Just as the shape of the earth is independent of what it is thought to be at any time or place.) Accordingly, it cannot be enough that the law is *thought* to be wrong: the question is whether it *is* wrong is relevant too.

Second, whether the case of civil disobedience is direct or indirect is relevant here. One's protest is, I think, more readily justified when it involves the breaking of a law that is thought to be wrong, rather than some other law. The reason is not complicated. In the case of indirect civil disobedience, the wrongness of the law serves as a reason for the *protest* against it. But in those cases of civil disobedience in which the law that is not obeyed is the same law against which the protest is made, the law's wrongness has an additional function as well. On the general grounds that one ought to do what is right and refrain from doing what is wrong, the wrongness of a law helps to justify *any* willing failure to obey it and since civil disobedience is not only protest but also disobedience, the wrongness of the law plays a dual role in the justification of direct civil disobedience.

2. *The purity and strength of the motive.* It is perfectly possible to believe a law to be wrong but to act against it for self-seeking reasons. "Of course it is a bad law," someone might think, "but I will protest against it because it reduces my income." If one is to be genuinely engaged in civil disobedience, the act of protest must be performed *because* a law is thought to be wrong; the motive must be moral. Yet, it may very well be true that there is no such thing as an unmixed motive; thus, if there is to be justified civil disobedience, it must at least be *relatively* free of an admixture of self-seeking motives. Not only the desire for personal gain counts against the justifiability of an act of civil disobedience; there are other, more subtle, temptations: the desire for fame or revenge, or for the grateful thanks from the underdog, or the anticipation of that special pleasure that may come from breaking the law. The purer and stronger the motive for setting right a wrong, the more readily a person is justified in performing an act of civil disobedience.

But not always when we ask whether an instance of civil disobedience is justified are we interested in whether some—or any—particular *person* was justified in doing what he did. Frequently, our concern in justifying civil disobedience is with the act as abstracted from the individuals who perform it. Motives, thus, have no place in the discussion; we ask only the other questions relevant to the justification of civil disobedience. But to ignore motives in this way is not tantamount to remaining neutral with regard to them. We are not asking whether an act of civil disobedience is justified on the supposition that the motive of the person who performs it either is or is not moral; on the contrary, as we reflect about the justifiability of an act of civil disobedience, we *assume* that it is done for moral reasons, that the person was not simply hired, for example.

This is what we take as given as we go on to inquire whether the act can be justified with respect to the other considerations relevant to justifying civil disobedience.

3. *The foreseeable consequences of the act.* One's estimate of what the consequences of engaging in civil disobedience are likely to be in a particular case is relevant to the justification of that case. To begin with, it makes a difference whether or not there is a likelihood of the act's being successful in bringing about the desired change. But there is no simple relation between probability of success and justification. If one's aim in the commission of an act of civil disobedience is fundamentally utilitarian, it will be harder to justify it, if the chances of success in bringing about the desired change are poor or absent than when they are excellent. Perhaps rebellion is called for, perhaps acquiescence. Still, if success in changing the law is more or less ruled out, there remains both the possibility of the creation of a moral climate *favorable* to future success, as well as the danger of public reaction *against* the very cause of the persons involved. And, depending upon the degree to which the law is thought to be wrong, one is justified in acting with greater or lesser expectations of success. On the other hand, if the person who engages in civil disobedience does so simply in order to manifest his belief that the law is wrong (however much he may *also* desire that the law be changed), the likelihood of the law's actually being changed is not a relevant consideration to the justifying of civil disobedience. In short, the relevance of success to the justification of an act of civil disobedience depends in part upon the *kind* of moral motive that plays a role in the performance of an act of civil disobedience.

Other consequences one must consider are what the risks may be that individuals and groups will in one or another way be harmed. It is more difficult to justify civil disobedience when the danger of violence is great, when not only those actually disobeying the law, but also officers of the government and innocent bystanders are likely to be hurt. Furthermore, the consequences for those who propose to engage in civil disobedience must be taken into consideration. If the punishment for breaking the law can be expected to be extremely severe, the commission of civil disobedience (always assuming other things to be equal) is less justified, for we do have duties to ourselves as well as to others. And from the consideration of these consequences for bystanders and actors follows a corollary that seems paradoxical. Still, it is true that where the agents of the state—the police and the judiciary—are cruel and punitive in the extreme, civil disobedience is not likely to be justified. In Nazi Germany of 1940, say, civil disobedience would have been pathetically inappropriate: a certain minimum level of civilization must be attained before civil disobedience can be justified; below it only evasion or rebellion—or acquiescence—are justifiable.

Finally, the more likely it is that the protest involved in civil disobedience can be confined to the law or measure thought to be wrong, the more readily can civil disobedience be justified. If there is in fact a clear danger that committing civil disobedience will spread to other laws, to lawlessness generally, or to a defiance of the state itself, then (again other things being equal) the justification of civil disobedience will be more difficult. For then what must be justifiable is not the single act of civil disobedience, but the lawlessness or revolution which is the likely consequence of that act. But the justification of this is a separate issue.

4. *The availability of alternative methods of reform.* It matters whether other techniques for modifying or revoking the law are available—for example, a cogent presentation at a public hearing. Civil disobedience is much more likely to be justified if the chances of change through legal means are remote.

Only an outline of what is involved in this question of alternative methods of reform can be included here. There are two broad classes of alternatives, the legal and the political; and in a society such as ours each has several modes. Both the federalist system and the system of common law provide more than one type of legal recourse in the case of a law thought to be wrong. And politically, the separation of the legislative and the executive functions alone means that there is more than one avenue of approach to the government, not to mention the many different techniques by means of which it can be subjected to pressure. Civil disobedience is more readily justified, the fewer alternative methods there are and the less likely it is that alternative methods will be successful.

It has been maintained that in a democracy, because there is always an alternative method and because success by legal or political methods is at least in principle always possible, civil disobedience is never justified. But this is surely false, for there are also the questions of probability and time. If the wrong is at all a serious one, the remote (in either

sense) possibility of change is not enough reason for denying the justified use of civil disobedience. It was Harold Laski who pointed out the absurdity of claiming that "the duty of a minority whose values are denied is the simple one of becoming a majority." The existence of alternative methods of reform is relevant to the justification of civil disobedience, but by no means to the extent of removing its possibility.

5. *Conscientiousness and evidence.* Whether what one takes to be wrong is indeed wrong, whether innocent bystanders are likely to be hurt, whether the community will respond to the moral claims being made, whether alternative methods of reform are likely to be successful, these and other similar questions are susceptible to a great deal of reflection and investigation. When we act, we can only act on the basis of what we think to be right; but recall that we can take fewer or greater pains to determine whether what we think to be the case is indeed so. For each degree of gravity of an undertaking there is a degree of conscientiousness that is appropriate. It would be silly to require a full-length study of possible consequences to help us to decide whether we ought to *eat out* or stay at home. But civil disobedience is a serious business: it goes counter to the general obligation to obey the law and almost always there are serious dangers of undesirable consequences for others. There is, therefore, a particular obligation to act conscientiously: to reflect carefully about all the considerations relevant and to bring oneself into possession of the best possible evidence pertaining to the many claims that are involved in *any* act of civil disobedience.

There is no doubt in my mind that many actual cases of civil disobedience, past and present, were justified. The injustice of the laws protested against was great; the motives of those engaged in the civil disobedience were as free of self-regarding admixtures as is possible among men; the various consequences that may follow from publicly breaking the law in protest were thought about and taken into consideration; alternative methods of reform were considered and found wanting. But above all, what distinguishes such men as Thoreau and Gandhi is the thoughtful way in which they reflected about the nature and ramifications of their acts. It is sometimes forgotten that one is justified in doing what one thinks is right only to the degree to which one is conscientious in trying to determine what is right. And because of the complexity of the act and the gravity of its consequences, this last consideration is of particular importance in justifying civil disobedience.

The Problem of the Compatibility
of Civil Disobedience with American
Institutions of Government

Charles L. Black, Jr.

. . . I am to speak on the compatibility of civil disobedience with American institutions of government. Now I am an American lawyer, a legal professional in one of the most legally-minded nations that ever existed. It will not surprise you to learn that my first raw reaction to this subject, several years ago, would have been that there is nothing in it at all. The incompatibility of civil disobedience with American institutions of government might indeed have been the subject of a speech, pithy and brief. Civil disobedience, such a speech might have run, is the defiance of law by someone who conceives that he is defying law in a good cause. The American idea is that law is established by the people through constitutional processes; that the change of law, even in a good cause, is to be committed to those processes; and that the yielding, by all, of obedience to law until it is so changed, is an invariable obligation. Therefore, civil disobedience never can be compatible with our American conceptions of orderly government.

Such would be the hardshelled lawyer's view, and it still seems to me to contain most of the truth. But when I see the civilized world united to honor those whom, on a first rough reading, this view might

Published originally in 43 *Texas Law Review* 492–525 (1965). Copyright © 1965 by the *Texas Law Review*. Reprinted by permission.

seem to condemn, and when I cannot deny my own feeling that it is the courage of these people that has been and is still the saving grace, not only of American life, but even of American legality, I am forced to examine this matter more closely, for what I may have missed.

And a deeper historical and cultural perspective reinforces this impulse. Passing the familiar examples of Socrates, Thoreau, and Gandhi, I think of a story of a young Pawnee brave, whose name comes back to me as Peshwataro. In his day the law of the Pawnee commanded that on the summer solstice there take place the sacrifice of the star maiden. A girl was each year captured from a neighboring tribe and bound to a stake. At dawn, the Pawnee braves would ride in a circle about her and shoot their arrows into her. This was not done for sport, but because, like so much that seems cruel in so many societies, it was thought to be a cruelty necessary to the maintenance of the moral and religious order. Many Pawnees, through what processes and influences I cannot say, came to disapprove of it and talked of doing away with it, but it was the law, and conservatism was too strong. Then one summer solstice at dawn this Peshwataro, a young man of high repute with the tribe, broke from the circle before an arrow was shot, rode furiously to the stake, freed the girl of that year, slung her in front of him, and escaped with her. He left her with her people and then rode back, much as Gandhi might have done, to submit himself to his fellows. As it happens, they did nothing. It was time, really, to stop this business; they had only needed an act of such courage to make that clear.

A case like that of Peshwataro forced me to conclude that the act of willful disobedience to law, while it never can be justified under law and, in that sense, never can be compatible with law, still may, though most infrequently, at the greatest crises exhibit a higher sort of compatibility with law, in that it may, if I may borrow from Professor Fuller a phrase which is both a philosophy of law and a poem about law, help the law in quest of itself. The exceedingly rare occasions on which a man of conscience and social responsibility could make this judgment are not, I think, susceptible of general definition. At least, many others have essayed such a definition and admittedly failed to find it, and I will stand with them. Two extreme and, to me, untenable positions ought to be mentioned.

The first is that a law need not be obeyed if it is unjust, that only just laws need to be obeyed. I cannot see what this can mean except that a law carries no obligation of obedience if the individual thinks it unjust, since the only communal standard that might be binding is *ex hypothesi* rejected, at least in a constitutional democracy, and in the absence of any overriding ecclesiastic authority. This view, in modern times, seems to have found its classic expression in Thoreau, though I confess that Thoreau is not wholly consistent, and would, moreover, yield much obedience for the sake of convenience, if not through a sense of obligation.

Now we common-law lawyers learn to control general expressions by reference to the context in which they occur. Thoreau spoke in the context of the operation of the Fugitive Slave Act in Massachusetts. A man was captured there; it was said that he was a slave. The man who claimed to be his master asked the aid of the federal power to return him to slavery. Slaves could be whipped and branded without effective controls. They could be sold away from their families. I think that my own serious thoughts about racism in America began here in Austin, when I was about seven years old, and listened to what at first I thought were the lover's sentimentalities of the song "My Poor Nelly Gray," and then I suddenly realized—perhaps by having it explained to me by someone who even then remembered—what the song meant, so that the world shook a little around me at knowledge of the horror that could disease the dealings of man with man.

If I had been alive then and had had the chance of saving a man from slavery by disobeying the law, I like to hope that I would have done it. In saying this, I necessarily confess my rejection of the second extreme position, that all laws ought to be obeyed, however cruelly unjust they may be. But I also think that Thoreau's general formula, that only the just law imports the obligation of obedience, is to be controlled by the context of readings in Frederick Law Olmsted, of routine plantation records of sale, of advertisements for runaways with brandings specified for easier identification.

Nor do I think that disobedience to the Fugitive Slave Law need have been committed with any wish that the whole legal order of the United States be destroyed, any more than Peshwataro, in performing his rescue, need desire or contemplate that his deed would bring the Pawnee order to the ground. It is perhaps the greatest paradox of political nature that the country that was home to one of the worst slaveries the Western world ever knew was at the very same time the last best hope of earth. One would have to understand almost everything—pehaps even things altogether hidden from man—to grasp how this could be. I note only that, so far as I can make out, this was the truth and that there are at least some circumstances under which I, and others like me, would make the choice of deliberately breaking the law without thereby choosing the death of the legal order.

I would reject, then, as facile and misleading, as altogether destructive of legal order, the notion that no one is obligated to obey any law he thinks wrong. I think I have said enough to show my belief that there may be circumstances, going far beyond a simple conviction of injustice, in which such disobedience is both justified and compatible with the general continuance of the legal order. Beyond this, I could only suggest factors to go into judgment: the clarity and magnitude of the evil, the hopelessness of remedy within the law, the possibility of disobedience without harm to innocent people, the probable efficacy of the act, the purity (as best one can assess it) of one's own motives, and doubtless others. Against all these have to be weighed, it seems to me, the almost but not quite irrebutable presumption that those who live under a system of law are to obey it even when they cannot square its commands with a private sense of justice. I doubt that the matter can be given much more clarity than this, unless one is prepared to accept one of the two very clear absolutist positions which to me seem untenable.

Up to now, I have been talking about the master-problem of civil disobedience as it is classically conceived, and I am afraid I have done little more than to exhibit that I think about this pretty much as the average man I am, and the far less-than-average philosopher. That the law is the law is an important thing indeed, and there is a mighty obligation of obedience. But this obligation, in the rarest of circumstances and after the gravest searching of soul, may have to give way to a mightier yet. What you will have observed is that all this presupposes, as most of the far more subtle philosophic discussions have presupposed, something called "the law," something called "the government"—a unitary and simple system, that is to say, of legal order and of legal obligation. And I am sure that what will have come into your mind is the thought that this is not our situation at all in the United States. Federalism exists elsewhere, but here it is the heart and soul of politics. We lawyers have come to expect that the most delicate questions in all parts of the law, from criminal justice to the labeling of food, from the racial discrimination to the financing of urban redevelopment, will arise from the fact that, over every person and over every square foot of our territory, except for a few special enclaves, two systems of law, two generating sources of legal obligation, exist—that of some state, and that of the nation. It would not be surprising to find that questions about what is commonly called civil disobedience are with us given a special cast by the existence of this federal system of ours. For the rest of my time, I propose to present two* principal reflections concerning the effect of federalism on the problem of what is ordinarily called civil disobedience.

The first reflection is one which you might think one could simply make and pass on. As William Taylor and others have clearly pointed out, much of what has lately been referred to, even by the actors, as "civil disobedience" is really not that at all. There is some evidence, however, that confusion still remains, and I would like to add a few words.

During the past few years, we have often heard the term "civil disobedience" used to describe the actions of persons who actively disobey local or state laws commanding racial segregation or who peacefully demonstrate to make plain and public their dispproval of this or some other racial discrimination. These people do, indeed, act in conscious violation of what is asserted to be legal authority, and they do offer themselves for arrest by the constituted authorities. But they do so in the belief, more or less clearly held and more or less clearly warranted, that the law itself is on their side and that the law's processes, in the end, will uphold them or will fail to do so only through an error in law. They appeal, in our federal system, over the head of the law and authority of the state, to the law and authority of the nation.

A first instance may be the case of the Freedom Riders of the summer of 1961. Most of these people were guilty of the offenses of riding unsegregated on interstate journeys, of standing about together unsegregated in waiting rooms, and of seeking unsegregated service in the station restaurants of interstate bus lines and railroads. There was a flavor of disobedience to law about all this, both because state and local statutes and ordinances forbade it and because local authorities—sometimes

---

*Only the first of those reflections is included here.—Eds.

applying a legal epithet, such as breach of the peace, that confused only if one desired to be confused—sought to punish it by legal processes. But there was not the faintest real doubt that the ordinances were void under federal law and that punishment of conduct protected by federal law cannot be justified in law by calling that conduct by some name that hopefully carries the inference of punishability. By and large, the Freedom Rides were instances of conduct clearly lawful, and the defiance of law was all on the other side.

The sit-in cases in establishments not directly in the stream of interstate commerce and not at the time subjected to federal statutory regulation present a different picture. Whether the federal constitution protects the right peaceably to remain on one's stool at a public lunch-counter after one has been refused service and asked to leave in obedience to a custom of segregation is a question of real difficulty. The point of law at issue, I remind you, is in that most storm-vexed field of law, the field of "state action." The guarantees of the fourteenth amendment, run only against actions of the states, and in the sit-in cases the immediate decision to discriminate was that of the proprietor. On the other hand, what the fourteenth amendment forbids a state to do is to "deny" equal protection of the laws, a form of words which surely imports some affirmative obligation, though its contours are not yet worked out. It can be contended that the custom of segregation to which the segregating proprietor conforms has for so many decades been supported by state law and policy that state power must be held a part of the causation behind individual acts taken in conformance to the custom. It would perhaps have surprised the sit-inners, in the total ambient, to learn that state power was to no significant extent involved in the segregation pattern to which they were being subjected; indeed, as a personal opinion, I am inclined to think it will surprise historians of the period to learn that this contention was so seriously urged and taken so seriously.

But the ultimate legal question is, by all objective indices, genuinely doubtful. The Supreme Court has split on it, three to three to three. The scholarly community is split on it. And we may never have an authoritative settlement from the Court because the Civil Rights Act of 1964 would seem now to furnish a complete statutory defense to the sit-inner and so to make moot the question of the impact of the fourteenth amendment considered alone.

The point, when we come to evaluate the act of the sit-inner, is that he usually acted under a claim of legal right, a claim not virtually certain of validity, as with the Freedom Riders, but tenable at the least and put forward in good faith. This is not to say that the children who marched into town to put their courage up against three centuries of prejudice did so while holding in their minds a clear legal theory, or several clear legal theories, on the "state action" problem; but they did, by and large, come in with the belief that they were in the right—in the legal as well as in the moral right.

The point may be made clear by a contrast between the respective acts of John Hampden and Henry Thoreau. The disobedience of each consisted in a refusal to pay taxes, one of the most purely passive but at the same time one of the most radically subversive of civil disobediences. But Thoreau took his stand, not on the ground that under law the tax was not owing, but on the ground that as a matter of moral choice quite outside the realm of legality he preferred and indeed felt bound to withhold his support from a government that enforced slavery. Hampden, on the other hand, withheld payment on the ground that the shipmoney as a matter of law was not owing. The sit-inners, in the main, are with Hampden.

In all cases, great or small, there is an element of claimed legal right and hence of an implied submission to rather than defiance of the order of law. There is, usually, a strong admixture of a moral in addition to a legal claim; the thing combatted, as in Montgomery, is felt to be wrong as well as unlawful. Nor is the legal claim always clear or even explicit; it is likely, for example, that the lady whose refusal to move back in the bus set the Montgomery movement going was consciously motivated rather by a realization that the request was an affront to her humanity than by an apprehension that her legal rights were being violated. But even this, the extremest case, the case of the person protesting injustice without thought to law, but under circumstances which do in fact found a tenable (and in her case a valid) legal claim, is very far indeed from the case of pure civil disobedience, of considered disobedience to what is known to be valid law under the applicable legal system.

Now I am reminding you, first, that very little in the last years' protest against racial injustice, that no major component in that protest up to now, bears the character of disobedience to law. Secondly, it seems plain, as to the future, that there is an enormous scope for the same sort of protest within the framework of law. Two over-arching guarantees are precisely applicable and vast in extension. The equal protection clause of the fourteenth amendment makes unlawful any racial discrimination that has in it a component of state power. And the federal guarantees of free expression throw the sanction of law around expressions of protest where these are unaccompanied by physical threat.

We now have, as well, the Civil Rights Act of 1964. It enlarges and clarifies the right to equality in many areas. Most important of all, in view of the vote by which it passed, in view of the circumstances surrounding its passage, and in view of other recent happenings, it may be taken to have fixed the national policy, stated the national consensus, as clearly and as firmly and through as many political organs as the Constitution makes possible. Courts do, because they should, take account of such a firm and broad fixing of policy in those tasks of interpretation and in those judgments of remedial wisdom which are necessarily committed to the judicial process. Segregation, for example, is now out of bounds in view of a unanimous Supreme Court, of overwhelming majorities in both Houses of Congress, and of the Presidency; nothing that could happen to fix this stone in place has failed to happen. The condemnation of apartheid is now among the most amply validated equities of federal law.

Why then does the aura of "civil disobedience" continue to surround assertions of the right to equality? Multiple reasons can be suggested.

First, the historical sources of the movement lie in Thoreau and Gandhi, each of whom actually faced the ultimate problem of resistance to law. Besides defying law, these two men acted nonviolently—Thoreau in a few single acts, Gandhi in carefully thought out and tested ways. It is this nonviolence, as a technique of struggle, that has actually been brought down and applied to the American racial conflict. But the engaged and busy men who have effected this have not always been careful to note, when their living of nonviolent resistance left them a little leisure for the statement of its theory, that their methods were not being employed in disobedience to law, but in the assertion and vindication of law under the federal constitution and the supremacy clause that makes the Constitution a law controlling the laws of the states.

In the phrase "laws of the states" lies a clue to another source of misunderstanding. In most of the racial protests and resistances, something which looks like law, which has passed through the legislature, which is printed where laws are printed, is being violated. It is easy to forget the supremacy clause and the underlying claim of federal legal right.

Thirdly, sometimes the person exercising civil disobedience elects not to appeal to the federal norm, but rather to acquiesce in the legality of the state rule and to take his punishment under that rule, so as to concentrate attention on the wickedness of the rule without any distracting considerations of federal law and so as to emphasize publicly his feeling of membership in the local community and his desire to seek conciliation at that level.

These three points are no more than explanations of a mistake, an important mistake to be sure, for it seems to confront the observer of racial protest with a philosophic and political problem he actually need not face, but a clear mistake none the less. A fourth explanation goes deeper. There is after all, it can be asserted, some functional similarity between true disobedience to law and disobedience to what was long thought to be law, to what is taken to be law still by many of the people concerned, to what is enforced as law by duly constituted authorities, even to customs so widespread as to be in some sense tantamount to law. To take Mr. Bayard Rustin's phrase, "social dislocation" on a very great scale is being brought about, and the dislocation in many communities is as great as any that would be brought about by some sheer disobediences to valid law. To undertake such dislocation is itself a grave matter. If every man and every group used all the room the federal law gave it to clash with local custom and local authority, the resulting dislocation would jar our states and our towns to the point of virtual fragmentation. Most of us are content to go along with local customs and local authority in most cases, insisting neither on our full federal constitutional rights nor on our own conceptions of propriety. The case for refraining in general from producing social dislocation reproduces in low relief the case for obedience to law. One must look, I should think, for a special moral urgency before deciding to insist on one's rights against strong community feeling, and the means adopted, it could be hoped, would be means apt to move the conflict toward a consensus, toward a new and better relocation, instead of widening it, insofar as such choice of means can consist with maintenance of principle. The structural similarity of these two considerations to those that might govern, respectively, the solemn decision whether law is to be disobeyed and what the mode of such disobedience is to be tends to result in confusion as to the nature of the norm disobeyed. Where the contemplation of social dislocation even in aid of law sends the mind to considerations so much like those raised by civil disobedience properly so called, it is perhaps natural that the two things, though so different in their ultimate placing in respect to the legal order, should be thought of as much the same.

So much for that part of civil disobedience which is not disobedience to law at all, but which is a solemn assertion of the nation's law against the law of some state, and which, far from being incompatible with our institutions, actually asserts and implements our law itself. . . .

The Obligation to Obey the Law

John Rawls

1. INTRODUCTION

I should like to discuss briefly, and in an informal way, the grounds of civil disobedience in a constitutional democracy. Thus, I shall limit my remarks to the conditions under which we may, by civil disobedience, properly oppose legally established democratic authority; I am not concerned with the situation under other kinds of government nor, except incidentally, with other forms of resistance. My thought is that in a reasonably just (though of course not perfectly just) democratic regime, civil disobedience, when it is justified, is normally to be understood as a political action which addresses the sense of justice of the majority in order to urge reconsideration of the measures protested and to warn that in the firm opinion of the dissenters the conditions of social cooperation are not being honored. This characterization of civil disobedience is intended to apply to dissent on fundamental questions of internal policy, a limitation which I shall follow to simplify our questions.

Originally presented at the meetings of the American Political Science Association, September, 1966. Some revisions have been made and two paragraphs have been added to the last section. Copyright © 1968 by John Rawls. Reprinted by permission of the author.

2. THE SOCIAL CONTRACT DOCTRINE

It is obvious that the justification of civil disobedience depends upon the theory of political obligation in general, and so we may appropriately begin with a few comments on this question. The two chief virtues of social institutions are justice and efficiency, where by the efficiency of institutions I understand their effectiveness for certain social conditions and ends the fulfillment of which is to everyone's advantage. We should comply with and do our part in just and efficient social arrangements for at least two reasons: first of all, we have a natural duty not to oppose the establishment of just and efficient institutions (when they do not yet exist) and to uphold and comply with them (when they do exist); and second, assuming that we have knowingly accepted the benefits of these institutions and plan to continue to do so, and that we have encouraged and expected others to do their part, we also have an obligation to do our share when, as the arrangement requires, it comes our turn. Thus, we often have both a natural duty as well as an obligation to support just and efficient institutions, the obligation arising from our voluntary acts while the duty does not.

Now all this is perhaps obvious enough, but it does not take us very far. Any more particular conclusions depend upon the conception of justice which is the basis of a theory of political obligation. I believe that the appropriate conception, at least for an account of political obligation in a constitutional democracy, is that of the social contract theory from which so much of our political thought derives. If we are careful to interpret it in a suitably general way, I hold that this doctrine provides a satisfactory basis for political theory, indeed even for ethical theory itself, but this is beyond our present concern.[1] The interpretation I suggest is the following: that the principles to which social arrangements must conform, and in particular the principles of justice, are those which free and rational men would agree to in an original position of equal liberty; and similarly, the principles which govern men's relations to institutions and define their natural duties and obligations are the principles to which they would consent when so situated. It should be noted straightaway that in this interpretation of the contract theory the principles of justice are understood as the outcome of a hypothetical agreement. They are principles which would be agreed to if the situation of the original position were to arise. There is no mention of an actual agreement nor need such an agreement ever be made. Social arrangements are just or unjust according to whether they accord with the principles for assigning and securing fundamental rights and liberties which would be chosen in the original position. This position is, to be sure, the analytic analogue of the traditional notion of the state of nature, but it must not be mistaken for a historical occasion. Rather it is a hypothetical situation which embodies the basic ideas of the contract doctrine; the description of this situation enables us to work out which principles would be adopted. I must now say something about these matters.

The contract doctrine has always supposed that the persons in the original position have equal powers and rights, that is, that they are symmetrically situated with respect to any arrangements for reaching agreement, and that coalitions and the like are excluded. But it is an essential element (which has not been sufficiently observed although it is implicit in Kant's version of the theory) that there are very strong restrictions on what the contracting parties are presumed to know. In particular, I interpret the theory to hold that the parties do not know their position in society, past, present, or future; nor do they know which institutions exist. Again, they do not know their own place in the distribution of natural talents and abilities, whether they are intelligent or strong, man or woman, and so on. Finally, they do not know their own particular interests and preferences or the system of ends which they wish to advance: they do not know their conception of the good. In all these respects the parties are confronted with a veil of ignorance which prevents any one from being able to take advantage of his good fortune or particular interests or from being disadvantaged by them. What the parties do know (or assume) is that Hume's circumstances of justice obtain: namely, that the bounty of nature is not so generous as to render cooperative schemes superfluous nor so harsh as to make them impossible. Moreover, they assume that the extent of their altruism is limited and that, in general, they do not take an interest in one another's interests. Thus, given the special features of the original position, each man tries to do the best he can for himself by insisting on principles calculated to protect and advance his system of ends whatever it turns out to be.

I believe that as a consequence of the peculiar nature of the original position there would be an agreement on the following two principles for assigning rights and duties and for regulating distributive shares as these are determined by the fundamental institutions of society: first, each person is to have an equal right to the most extensive liberty compatible with a like liberty for all; second, social and economic inequalities (as defined by the institutional structure or fostered by it) are to be arranged so that they are both to everyone's advantage and attached to positions and offices open to all. In view of the content of these two principles and their application to the main institutions of society, and therefore to the social system as a whole, we may regard them as the two principles of justice. Basic social arrangements are just insofar as they conform to these principles, and we can, if we like, discuss questions of justice directly by reference to them. But a deeper understanding of the justification of civil disobedience requires, I think, an account of the derivation of these principles provided by the doctrine of the social contract. Part of our task is to show why this is so.

3. THE GROUNDS OF COMPLIANCE WITH AN UNJUST LAW

If we assume that in the original position men would agree both to the principle of doing their part when they have accepted and plan to continue to accept the benefits of just institutions (the principle of fairness), and also to the principle of not preventing the establishment of just institutions and of upholding and complying with them when they do exist, then the contract doctrine easily accounts for our having to conform to just institutions. But how does it account for the fact that we are normally required to comply with unjust laws as well? The injustice of a law is not a sufficient ground for not complying with it any more than the legal validity of legislation is always sufficient to require obedience to it. Sometimes one hears these extremes asserted, but I think that we need not take them seriously.

An answer to our question can be given by elaborating the social contract theory in the following way. I interpret it to hold that one is to envisage a series of agreements as follows: first, men are to agree upon the principles of justice in the original position. Then they are to move to a constitutional convention in which they choose a constitution that satisfies the principles of justice already chosen. Finally they assume the role of a legislative body and guided by the principles of justice enact laws subject to the constraints and procedures of the just constitution.

The decisions reached in any stage are binding in all subsequent stages. Now whereas in the original position the contracting parties have no knowledge of their society or of their own position in it, in both a constitutional convention and a legislature they do know certain general facts about their institutions, for example, the statistics regarding employment and output required for fiscal and economic policy. But no one knows particular facts about his own social class or his place in the distribution of natural assets. On each occasion the contracting parties have the knowledge required to make their agreement rational from the appropriate point of view, but not so much as to make them prejudiced. They are unable to tailor principles and legislation to take advantage of their social or natural position; a veil of ignorance prevents their knowing what this position is. With this series of agreements in mind, we can characterize just laws and policies as those which would be enacted were this whole process correctly carried out.

In choosing a constitution the aim is to find among the just constitutions the one which is most likely, given the general facts about the society in question, to lead to just and effective legislation. The principles of justice provide a criterion for the laws desired; the problem is to find a set of political procedures that will give this outcome. I shall assume that, at least under the normal conditions of a modern state, the best constitution is some form of democratic regime affirming equal political liberty and using some sort of majority (or other plurality) rule. Thus it follows that on the contract theory a constitutional democracy of some sort is required by the principles of justice. At the same time it is essential to observe that the constitutional process is always a case of what we may call imperfect procedural justice: that is, there is no feasible political procedure which guarantees that the enacted legislation is just even though we have (let us suppose) a standard for just legislation. In simple cases, such as games of fair division, there are procedures which always lead to the right outcome (assume that equal shares is fair and let the man who cuts the cake take the last piece). These situations are those of perfect procedural justice. In other cases it does not matter what the outcome is as long as the fair procedure is followed: fairness of the process is transferred to the result (fair gambling is an instance of this). These situations are those of pure procedural justice. The constitutional process, like a criminal trial, resembles neither of these; the result matters and we have a standard for it. The difficulty is that we cannot frame a procedure which guarantees that only just and effective legislation is enacted. Thus even under a just constitution unjust laws may be passed and unjust policies enforced. Some form of the majority principle is necessary but the majority may be mistaken, more or less willfully, in what it legislates. In agreeing to a democratic constitution (as an instance of imperfect procedural justice) one accepts at the same time the principle of majority rule. Assuming that the constitution is just and that we have accepted and plan to continue to accept its benefits, we then have both an obligation and a natural duty (and in any case the duty) to comply with what the majority enacts even though it may be unjust. In this way we become bound to follow unjust laws, not always, of course, but provided the injustice does not exceed certain limits. We recognize that we must run the risk of suffering from the defects of one another's sense of justice; this burden we are prepared to carry as long as it is more or less evenly distributed or does not weigh too heavily. Justice binds us to a just constitution and to the unjust laws which may be enacted under it in precisely the same way that it binds us to any other social arrangement. Once we take the sequence of stages into account, there is nothing unusual in our being required to comply with unjust laws.

It should be observed that the majority principle has a secondary place as a rule of procedure which is perhaps the most efficient one under usual circumstances for working a democratic constitution. The basis for it rests essentially upon the principles of justice and therefore we may, when conditions allow, appeal to these principles against unjust legislation. The justice of the constitution does not insure the justice of laws enacted under it; and while we often have both an obligation and a duty to comply with what the majority legislates (as long as it does not exceed certain limits), there is, of course, no corresponding obligation or duty to regard what the majority enacts as itself just. The right to make law does not guarantee that the decision is rightly made; and while the citizen submits in his conduct to the judgment of democratic authority, he does not submit his judgment to it.[2] And if in his judgment the enactments of the majority exceed certain bounds of injustice, the citizen may consider civil disobedience. For we are not required to accept the majority's acts unconditionally and to acquiesce in the denial of our and others' liberties; rather we submit our conduct to democratic authority to the extent necessary to share the burden of working a constitutional regime, distorted as it must inevitably be by men's lack of wisdom and the defects of their sense of justice.

4. THE PLACE OF CIVIL DISOBEDIENCE IN A CONSTITUTIONAL DEMOCRACY

We are now in a position to say a few things about civil disobedience. I shall understand it to be a public, nonviolent, and conscientious act contrary to law usually done with the intent to bring about a change in the policies or laws of the government.[3] Civil disobedience is a political act in the sense that it is an act justified by moral principles which define a conception of civil society and the public good. It rests, then, on political conviction as opposed to a search for self or group interest; and in the case of a constitutional democracy, we may assume that this conviction involves the conception of justice (say that expressed by the contract doctrine) which underlies the constitution itself. That is, in a viable democratic regime there is a common conception of justice by reference to which its citizens regulate their political affairs and interpret the constitution. Civil disobedience is a public act which the dissenter believes to be justified by this conception of justice and for this reason it may be understood as addressing the sense of justice of the majority in order to urge reconsideration of the measures protested and to warn that, in the sincere opinion of the dissenters, the conditions of social cooperation are not being honored. For the principles of justice express precisely such conditions, and their persistent and deliberate violation in regard to basic liberties over any extended period of time cuts the ties of community and invites either submission or forceful resistance. By engaging in civil disobedience a minority leads the majority to consider whether it wants to have its acts taken in this way, or whether, in view of the common sense of justice, it wishes to acknowledge the claims of the minority.

Civil disobedience is also civil in another sense. Not only is it the outcome of a sincere conviction based on principles which regulate civic life, but it is public and nonviolent, that is, it is done in a situation where arrest and punishment are expected and accepted without resistance. In this way it manifests a respect for legal procedures. Civil disobedience expresses disobedience to law within the limits of fidelity to law, and this feature of it helps to establish in the eyes of the majority that it is indeed conscientious and sincere, that it really is meant to address their sense of justice.[4] Being completely open about one's acts and being willing to accept the legal consequences of one's conduct is a bond given to make good one's sincerity, for that one's deeds are conscientious is not easy to demonstrate to another or even before oneself. No doubt it is possible to imagine a legal system in which conscientious belief that the law is unjust is accepted as a defense for noncompliance, and men of great honesty who are confident in one another might make such a system work. But as things are such a scheme would be unstable; we must pay a price in order to establish that we believe our actions have a moral basis in the convictions of the community.

The nonviolent nature of civil disobedience refers to the fact that it is intended to address the sense of justice of the majority and as such it is a form of speech, an expression of conviction. To engage in violent acts likely to injure and to hurt is incompatible with civil disobedience as a mode of address. Indeed, an interference with the basic rights of others tends to obscure the civilly disobedient quality of one's act. Civil disobedience is nonviolent in the further sense that the legal penalty for one's action is accepted and that resistance is not (at least for the moment) contemplated. Nonviolence in this sense is to be distinguished from nonviolence as a religious or pacifist principle. While those engaging in civil disobedience have often held some such principle, there is no necessary connection between it and civil disobedience. For on the interpretation suggested, civil disobedience in a democratic society is best understood as an appeal to the principles of justice, the fundamental conditions of willing social cooperation among free men, which in the view of the community as a whole are expressed in the constitution and guide its interpretation. Being an appeal to the moral basis of public life, civil disobedience is a political and not primarily a religious act. It addresses itself to the common principles of justice which men can require one another to follow and not to the aspirations of love which they cannot. Moreover by taking part in civilly disobedient acts one does not foreswear indefinitely the idea of forceful resistance; for if the appeal against injustice is repeatedly denied, then the majority has declared its intention to invite submission or resistance and the latter may conceivably be justified even in a democratic regime. We are not required to acquiesce in the crushing of fundamental liberties by democratic majorities which have shown themselves blind to the principles of justice upon which jusification of the constitution depends.

5. THE JUSTIFICATION OF CIVIL DISOBEDIENCE

So far we have said nothing about the justification of civil disobedience, that is, the conditions under which civil disobedience may be engaged in consistent with the principles of justice that support a democratic regime. Our task is to see how the characterization of civil disobedience as addressed to the sense of justice of the majority (or to the citizens as a body) determines when such action is justified.

First of all, we may suppose that the normal political appeals to the majority have already been made in good faith and have been rejected, and that the standard means of redress have been tried. Thus, for example, existing political parties are indifferent to the claims of the minority and attempts to repeal the laws protested have been met with further repression since legal institutions are in the control of the majority. While civil disobedience should be recognized, I think, as a form of political action within the limits of fidelity to the rule of law, at the same time it is a rather desperate act just within these limits, and therefore it should, in general, be undertaken as a last resort when standard democratic processes have failed. In this sense it is not a normal political action. When it is justified there has been a serious breakdown; not only is there grave injustice in the law but a refusal more or less deliberate to correct it.

Second, since civil disobedience is a political act addressed to the sense of justice of the majority, it should usually be limited to substantial and clear violations of justice and preferably to those which, if rectified, will establish a basis for doing away with remaining injustices. For this reason there is a presumption in favor of restricting civil disobedience to violations of the first principle of justice, the principle of equal liberty, and to barriers which contravene the second principle, the principle of open offices which protects equality of opportunity. It is not, of course, always easy to tell whether these principles are satisfied. But if we think of them as guaranteeing the fundamental equal political and civil liberties (including freedom of conscience and liberty of thought) and equality of opportunity, then it is often relatively clear whether their principles are being honored. After all, the equal liberties are defined by the visible structure of social institutions; they are to be incorporated into the recognized practice, if not the letter, of social arrangements. When minorities are denied the right to vote or to hold certain political offices, when certain religious groups are repressed and others denied equality of opportunty in the economy, this is often obvious and there is no doubt that justice is not being given. However, the first part of the second principle which requires that inequalities be to everyone's advantage is a much more imprecise and controversial matter. Not only is there a problem of assigning it a determinate and precise sense, but even if we do so and agree on what it should be, there is often a wide variety of reasonable opinion as to whether the principle is satisfied. The reason for this is that the principle applies primarily to fundamental economic and social policies. The choice of these depends upon theoretical and speculative beliefs as well as upon a wealth of concrete information, and all of this mixed with judgment and plain hunch, not to mention in actual cases prejudice and self-interest. Thus unless the laws of taxation are clearly designed to attack a basic equal liberty, they should not be protested by civil disobedience; the appeal to justice is not sufficiently clear and its resolution is best left to the political process. But violations of the equal liberties that define the common status of citizenship are another matter. The deliberate denial of these more or less over any extended period of time in the face of normal political protest is, in general, an appropriate object of civil disobedience. We may think of the social system as divided roughly into two parts, one which incorporates the fundamental equal liberties (including equality of opportunity) and another which embodies social and economic policies properly aimed at promoting the advantage of everyone. As a rule civil disobedience is best limited to the former where the appeal to justice is not only more definite and precise, but where, if it is effective, it tends to correct the injustices in the latter.

Third, civil disobedience should be restricted to those cases where the dissenter is willing to affirm that everyone else similarly subjected to the same degree of injustice has the right to protest in a similar way. That is, we must be prepared to authorize others to dissent in similar situations and in the same way, and to accept the consequences of their doing so. Thus, we may hold, for example, that the widespread disposition to disobey civilly clear violations of fundamental liberties more or less deliberate over an extended period of time would raise the degree of justice throughout society and would insure men's self-esteem as well as their respect for one another. Indeed, I believe this to be true, though certainly it is partly a matter of conjecture. As the contract doctrine emphasizes, since the principles of justice are principles which we would agree to in an original position of equality when we do not know our social position and the like, the refusal to grant justice is either the denial of the other as an equal (as one in regard to whom we are prepared to constrain our actions by principles which we would consent to) or the manifestation of a willingness to take advantage of natural contingencies and social fortune at his expense. In either case, injustice invites submission or resistance; but submission arouses the contempt of the oppressor and confirms him in his intention. If straightaway, after a decent period of time to make reasonable political appeals in the normal way, men were in general to dissent by civil disobedience from infractions of the fundamental equal liberties, these liberties would, I believe, be more rather than less secure. Legitimate civil disobedience properly exercised is a stabilizing device in a constititional regime, tending to make it more firmly just.

Sometimes, however, there may be a complication in connection with this third condition. It is possible, although perhaps unlikely, that there are so many persons or groups with a sound case for resorting to civil disobedience (as judged by the foregoing criteria) that disorder would follow if they all did so. There might be serious injury to the just constitiution. Or again, a group might be so large that some extra precaution is necessary in the extent to which its members organize and engage in civil disobedience. Theoretically the case is one in which a number of persons or groups are equally entitled to and all want to resort to civil disobedience, yet if they all do this, grave consequences for everyone may result. The question, then, is who among them may exercise their right, and it falls under the general problem of fairness. I cannot discuss the complexities of the matter here. Often a lottery or a rationing system can be set up to handle the case; but unfortunately the circumstances of civil disobedience rule out this solution. It suffices to note that a problem of fairness may arise and that those who contemplate civil disobedience should take into account. They may have to reach an understanding as to who can exercise their right in the immediate situation and to recognize the need for special constraint.

The final condition, of a different nature, is the following. We have been considering when one has a right to engage in civil disobedience, and our conclusion is that one has this right should three conditions hold: when one is subject to injustice more or less deliberate over an extended period of time in the face of normal political protests; where the injustice is a clear violation of the liberties of equal citizenship; and provided that the general disposition to protest similarly in similar cases would have acceptable consequences. These conditions are not, I think, exhaustive but they seem to cover the more obvious points; yet even when they are satisfied and one has the right to engage in civil disobedience, there is still the different question of whether one should exercise this right, that is, whether by doing so one is likely to further one's ends. Having established one's right to protest one is then free to consider these tactical questions. We may be acting within our rights but still foolishly if our action only serves to provoke the harsh retaliation of the majority; and it is likely to do so if the majority lacks a sense of justice, or if the action is poorly timed or not well designed to make the appeal to the sense of justice effective. It is easy to think of instances of this sort, and in each case these practical questions have to be faced. From the standpoint of the theory of political obligation we can only say that the exercise of the right should be rational and reasonably designed to advance the protester's aims, and that weighing tactical questions presupposes that one has already established one's right, since tactical advantages in themselves do not support it.

6. CONCLUSION: SEVERAL OBJECTIONS CONSIDERED

In a reasonably affluent democratic society justice becomes the first virtue of institutions. Social arrangements irrespective of their efficiency must be reformed if they are significantly unjust. No increase in efficiency in the form of greater advantages for many justifies the loss of liberty of a few. That we believe this is shown by the fact that in a democracy the fundamental liberties of citizenship are not understood as the outcome of political bargaining nor are they subject to the calculus of social interests. Rather these liberties are fixed points which serve to limit political transactions and which determine the scope of calculations of social advantage. It is this fundamental place of the equal liberties which makes their systematic violation over any extended period of time a proper object of civil disobedience. For to deny men these rights is to infringe the conditions of social cooperation among free and rational persons, a fact which is evident to the citizens of a constitutional regime since it follows from the principles of justice which underlie their institutions. The justification of civil disobedience rests on the priority of justice and the equal liberties which it guarantees.

It is natural to object to this view of civil disobedience that it relies too heavily upon the existence of a sense of justice. Some may hold that the feeling for justice is not a vital political force, and that what moves men are various other interests, the desire for wealth, power, prestige, and so on. Now this is a large question the answer to which is highly conjectural and each tends to have his own opinion. But there are two remarks which may clarify what I have said: first, I have assumed that there is in a constitutional regime a common sense of justice the principles of which are recognized to support the constitution and to guide its interpretation. In any given situation particular men may be tempted to violate these principles, but the collective force in their behalf is usually effective since they are seen as the necessary terms of cooperation among free men; and presumably the citizens of a democracy (or sufficiently many of them) want to see justice done. Where these assumptions fail, the justifying conditions for civil disobedience (the first three) are not affected, but the rationality of engaging in it certainly is. In this case, unless the costs of repressing civil dissent injure the economic self-interest (or whatever) of the majority, protest may simply make the position of the minority worse. No doubt as a tactical matter civil disobedience is more effective when its appeal coincides with other interests, but a constitutional regime is not viable in the long run without an attachment to the principles of justice of the sort which we have assumed.

Then, further, there may be a misapprehension about the manner in which a sense of justice manifests itself. There is a tendency to think that it is shown by professions of the relevant principles together with action of an altruistic nature requiring a considerable degree of self-sacrifice. But these conditions are obviously too strong, for the majority's sense of justice may show itself simply in its being unable to undertake the measures required to suppress the minority and to punish as the law requires the various acts of civil disobedience. The sense of justice undermines the will to uphold unjust institutions and so a majority despite its superior power may give way. It is unprepared to force the minority to be subject to injustice. Thus, although the majority's action is reluctant and grudging, the role of the sense of justice is nevertheless essential, for without it the majority would have been willing to enforce the law and to defend its position. Once we see the sense of justice as working in this negative way to make established injustices indefensible, then it is recognized as a central element of democratic politics.

Finally, it may be objected against this account that it does not settle the question of who is to say when the situation is such as to justify civil disobedience. And because it does not answer this question, it invites anarchy by encouraging every man to decide the matter for himself. Now the reply to this is that each man must indeed settle this question for himself, although he may, of course, decide wrongly. This is true on any theory of political duty and obligation, at least on any theory compatible with the principles of a democratic constitution. The citizen is responsible for what he does. If we usually think that we should comply with the law, this is because our political principles normally lead to this conclusion. There is a presumption in favor of compliance in the absence of good reasons to the contrary. But because each man is responsible and must decide for himself as best he can whether the circumstances justify civil disobedience, it does not follow that he may decide as he pleases. It is not by looking to our personal interests or to political allegiances narrowly construed, that we should make up our mind. The citizen must decide on the basis of the principles of justice that underlie and guide the interpretation of the constitution and in the light of his sincere conviction as to how these principles should be applied in the circumstances. If he concludes that conditions obtain which justify civil disobedience and conducts himself accordingly, he has acted conscientiously and perhaps mistakenly, but not in any case at his convenience.

In a democratic society each man must act as he thinks the principles of political right require him to. We are to follow our understanding of these principles, and we cannot do otherwise. There can be no morally binding legal interpretation of these principles, not even by a supreme court or legislature. Nor is there any infallible procedure for determining what or who is right. In our system the Supreme Court, Congress, and the President often put forward rival interpretations of the Constitution. Although the Court has the final say in settling any particular case, it is not immune from powerful political influence that may change its reading of the law of the land. The Court presents its point of view by reason and argument; its conception of the Constitution must, if it is to endure, persuade men of its soundness. The final court of appeal is not the Court, or Congress, or the President, but the electorate as a whole.[5] The civilly disobedient appeal in effect to this body. There is no danger of anarchy as long as there is a sufficient working agreement in men's conceptions of political justice and what it requires. That men can achieve such an understanding when the essential political liberties are maintained is the assumption implicit in democratic institutions. There is no way to avoid entirely the risk of devisive strife. But if legitimate civil disobedience seems to threaten civil peace, the responsibility falls not so much on those who protest as upon those whose abuse of authority and power justifies such opposition.

NOTES

1. By the social contract theory I have in mind the doctrine found in Locke, Rousseau, and Kant. I have attempted to give an interpretation of this view in "Justice as Fairness," *Philosophical Review* (April, 1958); "Justice and Constitutional Liberty," *Nomos*, VI (1963); "The Sense of Justice," *Philosophical Review* (July 1963).

2. On this point see A E. Murphy's review of Yves Simon's *The Philosophy of Democratic Government* (1951) in the *Philosophical Review* (April 1952).

3. Here I follow H. A. Bedau's definition of civil disobedience. See his "On Civil Disobedience," *Journal of Philosophy* (October, 1961).

4. For a fuller discussion of this point to which I am indebted, see Charles Fried, "Moral Causation," *Harvard Law Review* (1964).

5. For a presentation of this view to which I am indebted, see A. M. Bickel, *The Least Dangerous Branch* (Indianapolis, 1962), especially chapters 5 and 6.

Rawls and Civil Disobedience

Peter Singer

This is an appropriate point at which to consider the theory of civil disobedience proposed by John Rawls in his much-discussed book, *A Theory of Justice*,[1] for Rawls's conception of the proper role of disobedience in a constitutional democracy has much in common with the kind of disobedience we have just been discussing. According to Rawls, civil disobedience is an act which "addresses the sense of justice of the community and declares that in one's considered opinion the principles of social co-operation among free and equal men are not being respected."[2] Civil disobedience is here regarded as a form of address, or an appeal. Accordingly Rawls comes to conclusions similar to those I have reached about the form which such disobedience should take. It should, he says, be non-violent and refrain from hurting or interfering with others because violence or interference tends to obscure the fact that what is being done is a form of address. While civil disobedience may "warn and admonish, it is not itself a threat." Similarly, to show sincerity and general fidelity to law, one should be completely open about what one is doing, willing to accept the legal consequences of one's act.

I am therefore in agreement with Rawls on the main point: limited disobedience, far from being incompatible with a genuinely democratic form of government, can have an important part to play as a justifiable form of protest. There are, however, some features of Rawls's position which I cannot accept. These features derive from the theory of justice which is the core of the book. The reader may have noticed that the sentence I quoted above contains a reference to "the sense of justice of the community" and to the "principles of social cooperation among free and equal men." Rawls's justification of civil disobedience depends heavily on the idea that a community has a sense of justice which is a single sense of justice on which all can agree, at least in practice if not in all theoretical details. It is the violation of this accepted basis of society which legitimates disobedience. To be fair to Rawls, it must be said that he is not maintaining that men ever do or did get together and agree on a sense of justice, and on the principles of social co-operation. Rather the idea is that a basically just society will have a sense of justice that corresponds to the principles that free and equal men would have chosen, had they met together to agree, under conditions designed to ensure impartiality, to abide by the basic principles necessary for social co-operation. It should also be said that Rawls does not maintain that every society in fact has such a sense of justice, but he intends his theory of disobedience to apply only to those that do. (As an aside, he suggests that the wisdom of civil disobedience will be problematic when there is no common conception of justice, since disobedience may serve only to rouse the majority to more repressive measures.)[3]

This is not the place to discuss Rawls's theory of justice as a whole. I want to discuss only its application to our topic. From his view that civil disobedience is justified by "the principles of justice which regulate the constitution and social institutions generally," Rawls draws the consequence that "in justifying civil disobedience one does not appeal to principles of personal morality or to religious doctrines . . . Instead one invokes the commonly shared conception of justice which underlies the political order."[4]

Even bearing in mind that this is intended to apply only to societies in which there is a common conception of justice, one can see that this is a serious limitation on the grounds on which disobedience can be justified. I shall suggest two ways in which this limitation could be unreasonable.

Firstly, if disobedience is an appeal to the community, why can it only be an appeal which invokes principles which the community already accepts? Why could one not be justified in disobeying in order to ask the majority to alter or extend the shared conception of justice? Rawls might think that it could never be necessary to go beyond this shared conception, for the shared conception is broad enough to contain all the principles necessary for a just society. Disobedience, he would say, can be useful to ensure that society does not depart too seriously from this shared conception, but the conception itself is unimpeachable. The just society, on this view, may be likened to a good piece of machinery: there may occasionally be a little friction, and some lubrication will then be necessary but the basic design needs no alteration.

Now Rawls can, of course, make this true by definition. We have already seen that he intends his theory of disobedience to apply only to societies which have a common conception of justice. If Rawls means by this that his theory applies only when the shared conception of justice encompasses all the legitimate claims that anyone in the society can possibly make, then it follows that no disobedience which seeks to extend or go beyond the shared conception of justice can be legitimate. Since this would follow simply in virtue of how Rawls had chosen to use the notion of a shared conception of justice, however, it would be true in a trivial way, and would be utterly unhelpful for anyone wondering whether he would be justified in disobeying in an actual society.

If Rawls is to avoid this trivializing of his position it would seem that he must be able to point to at least some societies which he thinks have an adequate sense of justice. This course would invite our original question: why will disobedience be justified only if it invokes this particular conception of justice? This version of the theory elevates the conception of justice at present held by some society or societies into a standard valid for all time. Does any existing society have a shared conception of justice which cannot conceivably be improved? Maybe we cannot ourselves see improvements in a particular society's conception of justice, but we surely cannot rule out the possibility that in time it may appear defective, not only in its application, but in the fundamentals of the conception itself. In this case, disobedience designed to induce the majority to rethink its conception of justice might be justified.

I cannot see any way in which Rawls can avoid one or other of these difficulties. Either his conception of justice is a pure ideal, in which case it does not assist our real problems, or it unjustifiably excludes the use of disobedience as a way of making a radical objection to the conception of justice shared by some actual society.

Rawls's theory of civil disobedience contains a second and distinct restriction on the grounds of legitimate disobedience. As we have seen, he says that the justification of disobedience must be in terms of justice, and not in terms of "principles of personal morality or religious doctrine." It is not clear exactly what this phrase means, but since Rawls opposes it to "the commonly shared conception of justice which underlies the political order" we may take it to include all views that are not part of this shared conception. This makes it a substantial restriction, since according to Rawls there are important areas of morality which are outside the scope of justice. The theory of justice is, he says, "but one part of a moral view."[5] As an example of an area of morality to which justice is inapplicable, Rawls instances our relations with animals. It is, he says, wrong to be cruel to animals, although we do not owe them justice. If we combine this view with the idea that the justification of civil disobedience must be in terms of justice, we can see that Rawls is committed to holding that no amount of cruelty to animals can justify disobedience. Rawls would no doubt admit that severe and widespread cruelty to animals would be a great moral evil, but his position requires him to say that the licensing, or even the promotion of such cruelty by a government (perhaps to amuse the public, or as is more likely nowadays, for experimental purposes) could not possibly justify civil disobedience, whereas something less serious would justify disobedience if it were contrary to the shared conception of justice. This is a surprising and I think implausible conclusion. A similar objection could be made in respect of any other area of morality which is not included under the conception of justice. Rawls does not give any other examples, although he suggests (and it is implied by his theory of justice) that our dealings with permanent mental defectives do not come under the ambit of justice.[6]

So far I have criticized Rawls's theory of disobedience because of certain restrictions it places on the kind of reason which can justify disobedience. My final comment is different. Rawls frequently writes as if it were a relatively simple matter to determine whether a majority decision is just or unjust. This, coupled with his view that the community has a common conception of justice, leads him to underestimate the importance of a settled, peaceful method of resolving disputes. It could also lead one to the view that there are cases in which the majority is clearly acting beyond its powers, that is, that there are areas of life in which the decision-procedure is entirely without weight, for instance, if it tries to restrict certain freedoms. (This view is similar to that discussed earlier in connection with rights.) Consider the following passage:

> It is assumed that in a reasonably just democratic regime there is a public conception of justice by reference to which citizens regulate their political affairs and interpret the constitution. The persistent and deliberate violation of the basic principles of this conception over any extended period of time, especially the infringement of the fundamental equal liberties, invites either submission or resistance. By engaging in civil disobedience a minority forces the majority to consider whether it wished to have its actions construed in this way, or whether, in view of the common sense of justice, it wishes to acknowledge the legitimate claims of the minority.[7]

There will, of course, be some instances in a society when the actions of the majority can only be seen as a deliberate violation for selfish ends of basic principles of justice. Such actions do "invite submission or resistance." It is a mistake, though, to see these cases as in any way typical of those disputes which lead people to ask whether disobedience would be justified. Even when a society shares a common conception of justice, it is not likely to agree on the application of this conception to particular cases. Rawls admits that it is not always clear when the principles of justice have been violated, but he thinks it is often clear, especially when the principle of equal liberty (for Rawls the first principle of justice) is involved. As examples, he suggests that a violation of this principle can clearly be seen when "certain religious groups are repressed" and when "certain minorities are denied the right to vote or to hold office. . . ."[8] These cases appear straightforward, but are they? Timothy Leary's League for Spiritual Discovery claimed to be a religious group using the drug LSD as a means of exploring ultimate spiritual reality. At least three other groups—the Neo-American Church, the Church for the Awakening, and the Native American Church—have used hallucinogenic drugs as part of religious ceremonies. Of these groups, only the last has legal permission to do so. Is freedom of worship being denied to the others? When is a group a religious group? There are similar problems about denying minorities the vote. Is the denial of the vote to children a violation of equal liberty? Or to convicted prisoners? It may seem obvious to us that these are legitimate exceptions, but then it seemed obvious to many respectable citizens a hundred years ago that blacks and women should not have the vote, and it seemed obvious to Locke that the suppression of atheism and Roman Catholicism were quite compatible with the principle of religious toleration.

When we go beyond religious persecution and the denial of voting rights, it is even easier to find complex disputes on which sincere disagreement over the justice of an action is likely to occur. Many of the issues which have led to civil disobedience in recent years have been of this more complex kind. This is why I do not think it helpful to assume that most issues arise from deliberate disregard of some common principles, or to try to specify limits, whether in the form of rights or of principles of justice, on what the majority can legitimately do.

NOTES

1. Clarendon Press, Oxford, 1972. The theory of civil disobedience is to be found in ch. 6, mostly in sects. 55, 57. and 59.

2. Ibid., p. 364.

3. Ibid., pp. 386-7.

4. Ibid., p. 365.

5. Ibid., p. 512.

6. Ibid., p. 510.

7. Ibid., pp. 365-6.

8. Ibid., p. 372.

Contributors

HUGO A. BEDAU (1926-   ), widely published in the field of social and political philosophy, is professor of philosophy at Tufts University.

CHARLES L. BLACK, JR. (1915-   ), Sterling Professor at the Yale University Law School, has written widely in the area of constitutional law.

PATRICK DEVLIN (1905-   ), a British lawyer who has held a variety of judicial positions in England, has published widely in the field of jurisprudence.

JOEL FEINBERG (1926-   ), professor of philosophy at the University of Arizona, is recognized for his published work in the area of contemporary moral and social issues.

ERICH FROMM (1900-1980), German-born psychoanalyst interested in philosophical issues, concluded his professional career as professor of psychiatry at New York University.

H. L. A. HART (1907-   ), professor of jurisprudence at Oxford University until his retirement in 1970, is well known for his writings in social and political philosophy.

LEON JAWORSKI (1905-1982), a practicing attorney for most of his professional career, served as president of the American Bar Association and was well-known for his role as Special Prosecutor in the Watergate case.

147

JOHN RAWLS (1921-   ), John Cowles Professor of Philosophy at Harvard University, is best known for his influential work *A Theory of Justice.*

PETER SINGER (1946-   ), professor of philosophy at Monash University in Australia, has written on a variety of contemporary moral issues.

RUDOLPH H. WEINGARTNER (1927-   ), a professor of philosophy at Northwestern University who is interested in Platonic studies and contemporary social issues, came to the United States from Germany in the 1930s.